Praise for *Never Apply*

"Where there's a way, there's a will. Most people don't lack the will to network, they lack the way. Once people find a way that makes sense, feels right, and is doable even by those who are a tad network challenged, they'll jump on it in a heartbeat. That is exactly what you should do with *Never Apply for a Job Again!* Don't leave home without it."
—Mark Goulston, author of the international best-seller *Just Listen: Discover the Secrets to Getting Through to Absolutely Anyone*

"*Never Apply for a Job Again!* is a provocative resource that not only hits the nail on the head about the importance of building and leveraging contacts and our network, but raises our thinking to do this *before* we need a job. It is a Protean approach…meaning we must take personal responsibility, anticipate, and adapt to a workplace in constant flux to land the job we want and deserve. Darrell Gurney's simple, easy-to-follow principles show you how to be proactive and successful in the new transformation workplace, where relationships reign supreme."
—Jay Block, best-selling author, international Protean career specialist

"I was very impressed. It has very clear and straight-forward advice to the job seeker. The principles are easy to understand and critical for gaining an advantage in this tough economy. As a whole, it addresses the secret of landing a job—employers hire people they like! In this book, [Gurney] tells us how to 'get liked.' Nice and short, with just the information the job seeker needs—no fluff!"
—Richard Knowdell, executive director of Career Development Network and author of *Building a Career Development Program* and *From Downsizing to Recovery*

"*Never Apply For a Job Again!* is what everyone needs to understand how the hidden job market works. Get it and use it before the secrets get out on WikiLeaks."

—Penelope Trunk, the original Brazen Careerist, author, blogger, entrepreneur

"In my best-selling book, I share the 5-10-15 Program as a way of staying active in networking. Coupling that type of regimen with the principles outlined in Darrell Gurney's *Never Apply for a Job Again!* cannot help but absolutely guarantee that anyone, anywhere can get the job of their dreams in almost no time. I strongly encourage every professional (self-employed entrepreneurs too), to read and incorporate these methods into your networking practice."

—Joe Sweeney, best-selling author of *Networking is a Contact Sport* and Milwaukee investment banker

"The reason most people stink at job interviews is that they are 'applying' for a job. Stop it! Cut the line, just find a way to help. Show people how you can make a difference for them. *Never Apply for a Job Again!* takes the philosophy of my work on Relationship Selling and puts it where it is most needed today: the job market. There is plenty of work for people who are willing to truly be worth their pay. Don't ever again sit in a human resources waiting room in hopes of getting hired. Just go help people grow their organizations."

—Jim Cathcart, author of the international best-seller *Relationship Selling*

"Darrell understands the essence of networking for your career or business. It's not about meeting as many people as possible. It's about really connecting, and then building and nurturing relationships with the right people. *Never Apply for a Job Again!* is essential reading for anyone looking for a new job or new opportunities."

—Dave Clarke, CEO of NRG Business Networks and writer of The Business Networking Blog

"Many job-seekers are lost in the sea of tactical career advice provided daily by blogs, job boards, and so on. As a consequence, these job-seekers spend their time following the herd instead of trying to change the odds in their favor by thinking and acting strategically. Darrell is one of the few career authors who force readers to do exactly that. *Never Apply For a Job Again!* helps job-seekers dramatically improve the probability of landing their dream job. Even better, the book prepares those already employed to get a head start in case of a future layoff. A must-read."

—Michael Froehls, PhD, management consultant, guest lecturer, and author of *The Gift of Job Loss*

"Who would not like to 'break the rules, cut the line, beat the rest?' Darrell wrote this book for job-seekers, yet it's excellent for all networkers. I think it's one of the best books I've ever read on the subject. I recommend it for anyone who wants good ideas for connecting with hard-to-reach people."

—Ken Tudhope, founder and CEO of Project Pro Search and author of The NetworkingNote.com blog

"I found the approach outlined in *Never Apply for a Job Again!* to be my own key to 'the collective intelligence.' It goes far beyond just finding a job, and I actually view the job part as a wonderful side effect of an amazing process. You have questions; this book will give you a way to get more answers than you ever thought possible. Happy reading!"
—Alex Marinescu, MBA, sales manager/general manager

"Powerful. Well written. Insightful. Real. A must-read for not only job seekers, but for everyone who strives to be the best they can be!"
—Debbie Ellis, master resume writer and president of Phoenix Career Group

"*I adore this book!* It is so entertaining and practical…and so helpful! This book is an essential read for insightful, witty, and bold truths about getting a job. Darrell coaches brilliantly, enabling you to cut the crap so you can get the job you love! I immediately adopted his fundamental philosophy: 'Meet and be known by others.' Anyone who implements these principles will be instantly shot out of the ballpark of competition and confidently on their way to a great job in this new economy."
—Bridget Nielsen, new grad, social media consultant, and passion coach

"Thank you so much for writing this book! My career experience includes approximately 20 years as a hiring manager, and everything in your book is spot-on. Now that the paradigm has shifted and I am the one looking for a job, it's hard to see clearly what needs to be done…so your step-by-step guide to the stealth approach is a lifesaver. I have moved emotionally from despair to enthusiasm, and now it's time to follow up with some action! So, quick success story: I have posted business ads on Craigslist many, many times to acquire consulting work and *never* got a single response. After reading your book, just for the heck of it, I posted an ad using some of your principles, and I got a hit: a real live potential client! A friend had just directed me to *What Color is Your Parachute?*, but I read your book first, and I am glad I did!"

—Levon Gagonian, customer service manager in career transition

"The content is true to the best experiences and qualities of human beings. It encourages people to strive for the best in themselves while bringing out the best and most human qualities of others...which includes the desire to help others. Anything that creates laser focus on reminding us of our true and best nature is eye-opening...and this book should open some eyes!"

—Richard Cornfield, president, Denali Film Group

"For very specific tactics on how to get unstuck in your job search, pick up this book. Mark it with a highlighter, and most importantly, implement the ideas from Darrell!"

—Jason Alba, author of *I'm on LinkedIn—Now What???*

"I highly recommend Darrell's approach, as he defines a new way to look at the job market. He has been successful with his clients, as the old ways of looking for a job are no longer valid."

—Terry Mills, president, NAACP, Corpus Christi, Texas

Never Apply for a Job Again!

BREAK THE RULES, CUT THE LINE, BEAT THE REST

By
Darrell W. Gurney

CAREER PRESS DISCARD

THE CAREER PRESS, INC.
Pompton Plains, NJ

NEVER APPLY FOR A JOB AGAIN!
EDITED AND TYPESET BY NICOLE DEFELICE
Cover design by Ian Shimkoviak / *The* BookDesigners
Printed in the U.S.A.

To order this title, please call toll-free 1-800-CAREER-1 (NJ and Canada: 201-848-0310) to order using VISA or MasterCard, or for further information on books from Career Press.

The Career Press, Inc.
220 West Parkway, Unit 12
Pompton Plains, NJ 07444
www.careerpress.com

Library of Congress Cataloging-in-Publication Data
Gurney, Darrell W.

Never apply for a job again! : break the rules, cut the line, beat the rest / by Darrell W. Gurney.

p. cm.

Includes index.

ISBN 978-1-60163-202-9 -- ISBN 978-1-60163-625-6 (ebook) 1. Job hunting. 2. Social networks. 3. Career development. I.Title.

HF5382.7.G87 2012

650.14--dc23

2011037721

Dedication

To my parents, Jewel and Larry,
who gave their best;

My son, Hunter,
who is learning and growing to be his best;

And my love, Rosario,
who brings out my best.

Acknowledgments

So many people to thank…along with so much apprehension that someone will be left out. But, as Yoda would say, "Courageously move forward, we must!"

From the outset, I'll first say thank you to all of the clients throughout the years who have surrendered their old paradigms about career change and job search to utilize this method and prove that it works. The results, and even miracles, that you have produced have been a source of great joy, satisfaction, and, oftentimes, amazement. I also want to thank all the seminar participants and guests from my talks who have asked me, for more than a decade, "Do you have a book on this philosophy?" That constant query is what finally had me sit down and outline the mindset and mechanics that resulted in this book.

I want to thank the now defunct career consulting firm of Bernard Haldane Associates where I was coached, at the ripe age of 24, on the ideas that formulated the beginning of this approach to career management, an approach I creatively expanded upon. The method, as I understood it then, allowed me to make an immediate demonstration of its viability when I landed my first corporate role in a competitive industry (entertainment) in a new city (Los Angeles) when I knew not a soul. Part of that thanks also goes to Jack Chapman, former head of the Chicago affiliate office of Bernard Haldane, for reminding me more than a decade ago of the body of wisdom I had learned and could, therefore, teach…in my own unique way.

Thanks goes out also to the career professionals who helped me expand from a 14-year career as a professional recruiter into the wider world of counseling and career development: Wendy Enelow, Susan Whitcomb, Debbie Ellis, Don Orlando, Randy Block, and the entire former Career Masters Institute group. I've also been blessed to have spent time with and learned from formative leaders and icons of the career industry: Richard Bolles, Richard Knowdell, and Martin Yate. I appreciate all the support and guidance that has been offered.

As for the actual coming together of this book, I want to thank the folks at Kingdom, Inc, and especially Andrea Davey, for help in creating the original eBook, under the title *Backdoor Job Search: Never Apply for a Job Again! 10 Time-Tested Principles for Launching an Effective Backdoor Campaign.* Next, I want to thank Rick Frishman for inviting me to his Author101 event where I met my agent, Bill Gladstone from Waterside Productions. Though I had engaged in previous interactions with Bill via e-mail—thanks to a referral by Erin Saxton—it was meeting face-to-face that moved that relationship into fruition (which demonstrates two major underlying principles of this book: referrals and face-to-face!). Thanks to Bill, what began as a simple eBook has now grown wings to carry the message further than it could have traveled by just sitting on my Website. Thanks also to Kathleen Rushall and Maureen Maloney at Waterside Productions: a great team.

I want to thank my "Web guy" out of Texas, Phil Drake, for all the support he has given me in the last few years to craft my message into the most cutting-edge Web form. I also want to thank the friends who helped me, all the way from the initial editing of the eBook to the designing of a title for this bookstore version: Richard Cornfield, Michael Hodge, Richard Knowdell, Debbie Ellis, Bridget Nielsen,

Beth Duerr Munro, Lisa Ermatinger, Shaun Baker, Allana Pratt, Angela Best, Barbara Anastasia, Brenda Anderson, Don Orlando, John Kremer, Dan Poynter, Alan Watt, Roz Esposito, Taffy Wallace, Stephanie Hubbard, Rafe Leyva, Marc Zicree, Scott Pitts, Mindi White, Agi Szecsenyi, Bryan Winter, Rick Hoppe, Shauna Markey, Craig Greager, Martin Cox, Rosario Zubia, and Joyce Sand.

Thanks to those who submitted stories about their experiences in using this method in their own career situations. I could only include a few, but appreciate the effort made by everyone, including Cathy Severson, Ron Feher, Ken Finster, Kay Stout, Connie Brizendine, Tessa Adler, and Randy Peyser. Thank you also to the creative handiwork of Rick Hoppe who stepped in with a customized CareerGuy graphic that filled a last-minute need perfectly. Thanks to Dan Lack, Sara Grace, Greg Bailey, Ann Longanecker, Erin Mellinger, Cathy Paper, Frank Wanderski, Jack Bennett, Linda Reilly, and Leann Little for helping with connections for endorsements…and thanks to all of those willing to bless this work with their endorsing words of encouragement. A big thank-you to Dr. Ivan Misner, The Father of Modern Networking.

I want to lastly acknowledge those closest to me, my mastermind group, my seminar transformation group, my Saturday support group, the wonderful woman in my life, and the emerging man in my life—my son. He recently landed his first job. Guess how. You got it: Stealth!

Darrell W. Gurney
Los Angeles, CA
www.CareerGuy.com

Contents

Part 2: 10 Time-Tested Principles for Launching an Effective Stealth Campaign

Foreword

For more than two decades, I have been working with business professionals and entrepreneurs across the globe, teaching them how to achieve significant business growth through business networking and referral marketing. Throughout the years, I have heard hundreds of amazing stories about the power of networking and what people have been able to achieve, not only in business, but also in life by simply building their personal network and making connections with others. I know of a million-dollar referral that was passed from a dentist to a logistics company after meeting at a networking event in Thailand, a couple who credits the successful adoption of their child to networking, several marriages that resulted from networking (including my own—I always say that my wife Elisabeth is the best referral I ever got!), and hundreds upon hundreds more stories testifying to the amazing results that networking can bring.

With this book, Darrell Gurney has painstakingly and effectively tailored networking's key concepts, strategies, and insights specifically to the needs of career professionals—individuals in the fields of accounting, marketing, operations, engineering, programming, and so on. Whereas entrepreneurs are often very inclined to get out and network, as they depend mostly on themselves to keep their business alive and thriving, career professionals can often adopt a false idea that they will be taken care of by a company and therefore don't always recognize the value of networking for their own advancement.

Never Apply for a Job Again! teaches not only entrepreneurs but also *the honorable and necessary professionals called employees* how to gain the top-of-mind awareness, affiliation, and opportunities that exist in abundance in our world—even in challenged economic times. A job is a job is a job, whether it's paid for by a salaried paycheck, a consulting fee, or a year-end dividend from the expansion of an enterprise. We all need our next "job," and Darrell Gurney's face-to-face method for climbing into the hearts and minds of people who matter is good, solid people sense. It's about high-*touch* when high-tech is all the rage.

People do business with people they trust, and they recommend these businesses to their friends. This same principle goes for career professionals, be they accountants, marketing folks, operations players, and even so-called "pocket-protector" techies such as engineers and IT experts: people stay connected to people they trust, and they recommend these people to others who can use their expertise by hiring them. Networking is, hands-down, the most time- and cost-effective strategy for landing your next opportunity, be it a long-term job or a temporary gig.

Stealth networking is the mainstream career management technique of the future. Career professionals who invest in themselves by learning how to stealth network like a pro will be rewarded with a long-term, sustainable, and stable career. As you peruse these pages, pay close attention to what is presented about stealth networking and building social capital—focus on building relationships and offering information that could be helpful to each contact you make, not in looking for a job. This way, there will always be a "somebody" out there who knows you and is referring you. The fact is, we're more interested in people who seem interested in us... it's a symptom of our me-centered culture. This is what Darrell teaches in Stage 1 of The 5 Stages of a Stealth Meeting— your complete and total focus should be on asking questions and being intimately interested in the person you're meeting with, his background, her industry history, and so on. Call it an act from the referral gods, but when you do good things for others, those good things have a habit of making their way back to you—even if from a different person or group of people. Build "relationship equity" just to build it and the universe responds. Take note of all that just arises "out of the blue": the former employer from years ago who just happens to call; the neighbor who tells a friend about you; the volunteer opportunity that has you working beside a CEO in your industry. By getting out and connecting, you fertilize and water your "out of the blue" garden.

Overall, Darrell Gurney's method is a great referral generation strategy. As I spell out in my book *Networking Like a Pro*, senior executives are hiding from you. Darrell shows the way to win at this game of hide-and-seek. You'll be shouting "Olly olly oxen free" all the way into the good graces of these senior players who will reveal themselves to you...to get you hired.

~IVAN MISNER, PHD, *NEW YORK TIMES* BEST-SELLING AUTHOR, AND FOUNDER OF BNI

Preface

My first book, *Headhunters Revealed! Career Secrets for Choosing and Using Professional Recruiters,* came out a decade ago. It was to assist job-seekers in getting the most value out of a viable tool of career transition—third-party recruiters, or *headhunters.* I wrote it during the late 1990s, a working world shaped by a candidate-driven market, when there were far more good jobs available than people to fill them. It was written from the perspective of having been a professional recruiter for more than 15 years, finding jobs for everyone from executive VPs, CFOs, and directors of sales to human resource managers, executive assistants, and accounting clerks.

Headhunters Revealed! basically asserts that it is always smart to have the career partnership of a headhunter in your back pocket when managing your career, in the short term ("I need a job NOW!"), and as a passive candidate in the long term ("If the right opportunity comes up, I'll consider making a move."). Knowing how to best work with these enigmatic entities, how they operate their business, and what makes them tick allows you to reap the most benefit from their expertise. In strong and vibrant economies, headhunters are a savvy supplement to your personal job-seeking efforts.

But recruiters, all the way from temporary clerical agencies to high-end, retained executive search firms, are just one tool in your job-seeker pouch. Also, they have a limited ability to help you in slow economic times—what is called an employer-driven market—because there simply aren't as many jobs to fill. When there is plenty of talent available in the market, employers can recruit more directly on their own and avoid placement fees. So, it is important to learn effective job search methods in order to become your own career manager. This skill is handy for all economic seasons, yet it's often the recessions that wake most people up to the need to learn new ways to approach their job search.

CareerGuy Tip: Become your own career manager, for good times and bad.

Only 20 to 35 percent of the entire job search spectrum lies within the public-knowledge domain. The rest, 65 to 80 percent, rests in what's called the "hidden job market." To take charge of your own career, and not rely on the whims of the market or other folks to do it for you, you must learn to tap into this hidden market—not just for your next job, but for life. In any economy, the person who knows how to connect with unadvertised, behind-the-scenes opportunities through building relationships will *always* come out on top. This book, *Never Apply for a Job Again!*, will assist you in doing just that.

Please note that if you replace the word *job* in the previous paragraph with the words *entrepreneurial opportunity* or *new client*, you'll realize that this method applies just as well to these ventures...because it's all just a "job" in one way or another. The point is, pursuing new clients or opportunities in the same way everyone else does is predictable, recognizable, and filterable. You'll want to use this same stealth approach to create many more career openings in those areas also. So, anywhere in this book that you see the word *job*, simply make that replacement.

In these pages, I will offer you the insight, philosophy, and instructions that I've provided for thousands of clients throughout my 25 years in the career coaching and recruiting business. You'll learn how to be in command of your own job search or other career movement through developing and maintaining professional relationships. Therefore, your "security" will no longer be dependent on any particular employer, recruiter, or even field, but will be placed firmly into your own hands.

I will first share with you the dirty truths about job-seeking from both overt and stealth perspectives, so that you are thoroughly convinced of the near senselessness of responding to ads. I will then show you how to effectively tap into the hidden job market through building connections with others—people you already know, as well as those you don't.

I'll have to alter your thinking first, so that you embody the necessary mindset to authentically create stealth relationships. But after a thorough brainwashing of your desperation and neediness, I'll show you specifically how to form these bonds, how to go from being a complete unknown to folks in positions of knowledge, power, and influence, all the way to becoming a connected and top-of-mind acquaintance—even colleague!

> *"The most effective career-enhancement tool since humans arrived on the planet: the good opinion and favor of others."*

Why to connect, whom to connect to, how to contact, where to meet, how to conduct the conversations, and the entire mechanics of maintaining the relationship after initial contact: I'll cover all of this and more to ensure that you can begin utilizing the most effective career enhancement tool since humans arrived on the planet: the good opinion and favor of others.

I am committed that, once and for all, you see that you can be in charge at all times of your own career movement. In empowering you to do so, my own life purpose of ensuring that people experience aliveness and freedom to create inspired new futures is satisfied. We've got this one life, and we spend one-third to half of our waking hours working. Let's make it count—for us, and for our world.

THE LITTLE BIT EXTRA... THAT MAKES A WORLD OF DIFFERENCE

Are you willing to believe that this little book can open up something completely new as possible in your career life?

Are you willing to have it not just be another tome of good ideas, most of which exit your mind as soon as you put it away?

I believe that the intention you include with the time you take to read and engage in this process will make all the difference in the world. For example, how many times do you read a book that has sections of questions for you to answer...but you don't answer them? How many helpful guides have given you an exercise to practice so that you can gain a new understanding of something...but you skip over it? The reason that coaching and consulting are such big businesses today is that, left to our own devices, we often don't put in that little bit extra that we would if we were face-to-face, in front of our coach, doing the tasks we're given!

Look, you can't expect to learn something without practicing, and you can't put sentences together until you've learned and rehearsed your ABCs. Therefore, I ask you (for your sake, not mine) to offer a really high intention as you move forward into this book so that you will do what it takes to have it make a difference for you. Having something at stake will make you play a whole different way.

In business and in life, we know that high return often requires high risk. Otherwise, anyone could have anything. Though I do believe anyone can have anything, it requires commitment and courage to really risk oneself to get it. What are you willing to put on the line to make happen in your life and career out of investing your time into this book and mastering this process? Is it a new job closer to home, doing what you really love, with folks you enjoy? Is it an entire career change, into a new field that you've only dreamed about? Is it your own entrepreneurial venture, in an area that you've pondered for so many years? What is it for you? Be really detailed about it.

If you go through this book casually, you'll have a certain result. However, if you declare upfront what you intend to create for yourself out of it—even if you have no idea now of how that would unfold—you'll go through the book differently. You'll actually *do* the exercises I give you! You'll actually *answer* the questions I pose. You'll be operating with something "at stake."

I promise you that, if you are willing to put something truly miraculous for yourself at stake, and do the exercises and answer the questions I give you throughout the book, something, absolutely *something*—even if it's only one simple nugget that you get—will undoubtedly make a huge difference in the way your career flows from this point forward.

Will you accept my challenge? Will you go out right now and get a special spiral notebook that you will dedicate to engaging in your career expansion throughout this book? Write on the front of it "My Career Transformation Insights Journal."

For the sake of what you are putting at stake, I invite you to act as though reading this book and doing this internal and external work will make things possible in your career that never were before.

For now, in order to give you the inspired support necessary to actually take this on, declare what you are putting at stake for engaging fully in this book.

I ask you to do this because I want you to affirm right now that you're willing to play this way, and thereby get yourself in action even before you have a chance to step away and forget this section. Sometimes the mere act of committing that a difference *can be made* in our life starts that difference happening.

Declaration: What I'm willing to put at stake for engaging fully in this book:

_____

_____

_____

_____

_____

_____

_____

I hereby solemnly swear I will have my "Career Transformation Insights Journal" by _____ (date) and be ready to move forward…so help me, *me*!

_____

Your Signature

PART 1:
RETHINKING AND RULE-BREAKING

Chapter 1: Rules to Start Breaking

As you move through this book and practically adapt the ideas, mindset, and methods offered to your own career situation, I want you to realize the underlying rules that these ideas, mindsets, and methods provide the opportunity to break. Some of these rules are ingrained from our childhood experiences and some are learned and implied by our respective life experiences. They may vary somewhat for each individual, but there's an underlying grain of each of them in our constitutional makeup. Otherwise, we'd still be operating as if we were 4-year-olds, out saying "Hi!" and talking to everyone left and right. Maybe you didn't do that as a 4-year-old, but I did...and I see that little kids have a *lot* more freedom to be in the world before they learn these rules.

At this point, let me introduce you to my "soapbox." As we work together, you'll see that I tend to get on a soapbox every now and then to emphasize certain points or to generally rant about your best career interests. So, we might as well get started here...

Rules Ingrained from Childhood Experience

Don't Talk to Strangers

What? Who said? Your mom when you were running around the grocery store talking to everyone and embarrassing her? There's no better time to forget that rule than right now. There's someone in front of you and someone behind you when you're in line for that latte at the coffee shop. You never know if one of those people happens to be the sister-in-law of your next employer, client, or business partner. Talk to people! Everywhere! Anywhere! Become a COW: Citizen of the World.

Mind Your Own Business

Does that mean just don't get involved? Don't step out and interject into a conversation you hear going on about something you're interested in or know something about? Never eavesdrop? Just stay in your world and "respect" others in theirs? Sure, if you want to ensure that you will always stay in your little world, go ahead: Play life that way. But, believe me, just like in Monopoly, you don't build up your properties as fast without dealing with the outer world of other players. Get out there! Offer your insight, show your interest, interject, and ask questions!

Wait Your Turn

That's what the good little boys and girls do, right? Or so your kindergarten teacher said. Bull! The folks who get what they want or where they want to go most often learn to *take* their turn. Now, I'm not saying be obnoxious and trounce everyone underfoot. But believe me, most people have a *long way to go* before they get to that extreme. Just be nimble, be quick, and go for it! Get your hand up first! Strategically look for spaces to step into. They're everywhere!

Play Fair

Your Sunday School teacher told you this was the way to behave, right? Well, I'm not advocating a lack of core ethics, but that childhood programming served to stomp out a lot of simply good entrepreneurial initiative in the way people operate. A favorite Ziggy cartoon of mine by Tom Wilson shows Ziggy asking, "If the meek shall inherit the earth, who is going to step up and claim it?" Ethics and meekness are two different things. How about "Play to Win…Ethically." Granted, the whole subject of ethics is another book, but hopefully you get the point. Look for and capitalize on an edge anywhere you can.

Don't Speak Until Spoken to

Maybe that was more of a 1920s or 1940s childhood reproach, but I still remember remnants of it around the dinner table in my early days! The point is, we were all taught, to some degree, to limit our communications with others, to stay in our space and respect each other's boundaries. That brainwashing has limited our openness to simply reach out and connect. When there's a big earthquake or disaster, we're all out in the street acting like brothers and sisters. Otherwise, we're isolated in our own little worlds. Reach out! Start a conversation with that doorman, barista, checkout clerk, bus driver, person next to you in the dentist's waiting room, or little old man sitting beside you on the subway. You have *no idea* who they may be or who they may know!

Don't Toot Your Own Horn

When have you ever seen someone grab a band member's instrument and start playing it for them? Never. It's *that* band member's responsibility. If you ain't tootin' your own horn, nobody is! And, if you have a special gift, talent, skill, or essence to offer the world (which I believe everyone does) *and you're NOT tootin' it*, it's a damn shame and an outright crime.

Don't Bother People

This is a major voice of early programming that ensures that "salespeople" will always have a special place in society—because they transcended this voice! Whether it was a busy parent we felt intimidated to make requests of or some particular incident that had us believe we were a nuisance, the idea that we shouldn't bother others took hold. The truth is that, outside of our deeply ingrained fears of rejection, we all *love* to interact and participate with one another! The point, yet again, is that folks live inside their safe little worlds and don't reach out or let in what could help. Your "bothering" someone to start a conversation with them in the line at the grocery store may serve to transfer some information between you that could be helpful. I'm not saying go out begging for what you need, or become the do-or-die Boy Scout forcing a reluctant old lady across the street. Just keep in mind that when we're out pointedly finding ways to interact with others, we discover resources, knowledge, and information that moves everyone forward. Plus, we have an opportunity to be continually amazed at the profound truth of the simple statement: "It's a small world after all."

Play by the Rules

Go back to the comments earlier about our childhood indoctrination to "play fair." You should always be asking yourself, "What are the rules I'm playing by? Who set them up? What are the rules attempting to control? Whom do the rules serve?" Although I'm not encouraging outright anarchy, stretching yourself to get outside the box of standard ways of thinking and operating with regard to your career can't help but move you forward. A big marketing guru (which you want to become in terms of your own career) named Dan Kennedy said, "Observe what the majority are doing, then do the opposite." Take this to heart in your career management and search for opportunities. Question authority! Become a contrarian!

The next lines that we want to get outside of are those implied by life experience, the supposed "lessons" we've learned, and ways of adapting that we've incorporated through the trials and tribulations of living life.

RULES IMPLIED BY LIFE EXPERIENCE

Don't Stand Out

Remember in third grade when you were so excited to raise your hand to answer, "Washington!" but the answer was actually "Lincoln"? Then you were laughed at, and decided, "I'll never, ever, ever stick my neck out again!" Maybe you didn't have exactly that experience, but trust me, somewhere in your life you decided to play it safe and not take a risk. We all do…and then the rest of our adult life is spent (if we're lucky) in an attempt to shake off the constrictions of our self-expression that we adopted so early on. To heck with that! Stand out! Get noticed! Be willing, within certain realms of decency and basic coolness, to break out from the crowd and do things differently, present yourself differently, and get noticed differently!

Stick With One Thing

Did you grow up with the idea that you were supposed to figure out what you were going to be in life and then stick to it? Did the adults (who supposedly had it all figured out) ask you, "What do you want to be when you grow up?" so often that you felt you had to figure it out? At 8 years old, a good friend of mine was found crying on his front porch by his mother. When she asked why, he said, "I don't know what I want to be when I grow up!" Of course, she told him he had plenty of time to figure that out. And, if you're like me, the older you get, you wonder even more what you want to be when you "grow up." Let go of the idea that it's already carved in stone what you *want to, need to, have to, should/ could/would be* in life! As you will learn, you have way more options than you think, maybe not inside your old mindset or your old way of connecting with the world…but that's why you're reading this book.

Don't Be Pushy

Did you ever let your excitement or anxiousness get the better of you, that you pressed a bit too hard? Did you nag for something so much that you were reprimanded? Did you then decide to simply stop asking in life? Well, the simple truth is, the answer for whatever you want in life is already *no* if you don't ask. Renowned hockey superstar Wayne Gretzky said, "You miss 100 percent of the shots you don't take." Whether it's a crack at a new field that you've always wanted to try, an industry leader you'd like to know better, or even increasing your consulting fees, you'll only receive into your experience what you're willing to allow yourself to accept, and asking is the first step to allowing. Be tenacious! With politeness, persistence is potent and downright miraculous.

Avoid Rejection at All Costs

Who knows where you or I picked it up individually, but the overall human experience trains us to stay in our own little world because we might get rejected. Think about it: isn't that why we don't still operate like 4-year-olds, playing full out, meeting and talking to everyone, treating the world like one big, whopping possibility? We get on subways, we crowd onto elevators, and we sit in coffee shops abiding by some group-consciousness agreement to keep to ourselves so that nobody has to risk the chance of not being liked by someone else. The idea of rejection is a possible interpretation of many of the events that occur in our life, but not the only interpretation. When we get a rejection letter, does it imply that we are not worthwhile human beings? When we are dumped, cast aside, or let go in a relationship or job, does it mean we are bad and wrong? No, those are all meanings that we add to these situations. There are other possible meanings we could ascribe. What if this is the universe saying to us that our better good is coming from somewhere else? Of course, as humans who resist change, we feel discomfort because some old prospect is going away, but that means something new is available to us. Many successful people went through what we could deem rejection until they arrived at their place of power. (Read about the life of Abraham Lincoln if you want an example.) Perhaps what we consider rejection is simply *redirection*. And this applies in situations as simple as saying hello and conversing with someone you don't know. If that person isn't as fluid yet in their openness to interacting with strangers, nor as aware (as you are becoming) of the absolute wealth of connections, information, and resources around each of us at all times, and they run away when you try to start a conversation with them, that's not *your* problem. Maybe one day they will open up…but *your* job is to keep getting outside of *your* box, *your* rejection-phobic ways of operating, and to generate connections with others.

Do Things the "Right" Way

Perhaps you once made a mistake when trying something new, and you were called out on it. Or maybe you once made a choice that, in retrospect, you think was a wrong one. Whatever the case, many of us live inside self-imposed pressure to only do things if we can do them "right." Yet, often, the mere idea of "right" is completely subjective and open to interpretation. Was it "right" that Bill Gates became a college dropout at age 20? Was it "right" for Mark Zuckerberg to create Facemash while at Harvard, causing the administration to reprimand him for crashing the university servers and upsetting many of his fellow students by using their pictures without permission? Being in action to do things, even without knowing the "right" way to do them, at least gets you in the game of learning more and following your unique path. Sure, some prudent planning ahead may be helpful, and yet the following command will often get you closer to your dreams: "READY! FIRE! AIM!" In other words, don't wait until you can always see your target with analytical and perfectionistic accuracy. Take a shot!

Don't Ask for Favors

There's an inner squelch mechanism that holds most of us back from asking for what we want. Some folks would just sit with a bad meal at a restaurant rather than send it back and get something else. A friend and I once agreed that, whenever we offered to do something for each other (for example, "Can I make you a sandwich?"), we could never say no or "Oh, don't go to that trouble." We had to absolutely accept whatever was offered by the other. This practice flew in the face of the natural human tendency to think we're putting people out or creating an inconvenience when they do something for us. But think about it: Don't you like the feeling when you've helped someone out? Most of us *love* it! Then why would you be so stingy as to not let another person experience that same feeling? Sometimes the biggest contribution you can make to someone is letting them contribute to you. Ask! Give someone the good feeling of contribution by letting them do something for you!

Important People Don't Have Time For Me

Remember the caste system in high school? Where did you fit in? Were you one of the cool, "in" crowd? Were you one of the band dorks? Were you a geek? A jock? Mr. or Ms. Goody Two-Shoes? The brainiac? Was it "better" to be one or the other? We learned early in life, and often still believe, that someone is better or more important because of some social or corporate stature that they hold. Those folks may even *want* us to think of them that way, which is why they ascended to their throne. However, underneath it all, we all put on our pants one leg at a time, we all have issues, and we all have our challenges. There's nobody intrinsically more important than anyone. There's just who we can make time for, given the hustle and bustle of our individual lives. We always make time for that which speaks to us at some deep level of our being. Therefore, it's never a question of someone's relative importance as to whether they will take time for you. It's simply a question of you finding a way to speak to some deep level of their being. You are just as important as anyone…and your job is to find ways for people to discover your importance to them.

Follow the Proper Channels

Akin to the admonishment to "stay within the lines" that we all heard when coloring, this rule will defeat you in your job search or opportunity cultivation every time. Look, investors make gobs of money all the time on insider information! Stephen Spielberg started his career by dressing in a black suit, carrying a briefcase, and strolling past security guards at Universal Studios for months to get inside and get known by people. As I said earlier, you can "play by the rules" developed to control the masses, or you can become innovative and adventurous. For sure, the "proper" channels of job search have you competing head-to-head with thousands of desperate and needy folks. Do you think that's wise? Get strategic!

So, I'll step off of my soapbox for now, encouraging you to think differently or rethink your ways of getting where you want to go. Break the rules! Cut the line! Beat the rest!

Chapter 2:
Why Applying for a
Job Is Dumb

My earliest career moves were shaped by a career transition method and mindset that I coined The Stealth Job Search Method. I learned it at age 24, within a couple months of arriving in Los Angeles. I showed up in Tinseltown knowing nobody, and, like every other starry-eyed import, wanted to get into the entertainment business. I had degrees in finance and international business, and had worked for a Big Eight accounting firm in London, England, for a year after college. I wanted to land a role in a major studio, and realizing that so many other folks did too, I decided I would have to be competitively unique. So, I hired a career coaching firm to assist me.

They taught me a method of connecting with people in my area of interest and, utilizing it, I personally met seven CFOs of the top entertainment studios in their offices within two months. In one of those meetings, never having met that CFO before, I left a couple hours later having just been hired into the international financial division of MGM/United

Artists—without Human Resources (HR) even knowing my name yet! I tweaked that method throughout many years, and have now coached hundreds of folks on using it for effective (and fun!) career transitions.

AN OVERT FOLLY, A STEALTH BONANZA

I have found that most people are neither aware of nor properly utilize a stealth approach in managing their career movement. Here's exactly *WHY* you want to learn this method.

First, let me pose to you a few questions:

1. When you apply for a job that you've seen posted online or somewhere else, just how many other people do you think may have seen and applied for that same position? Just you? A few more? A few hundred more? Many more than that?

2. What makes you think your application or resume is going to stand out from the others? Just how much time do you expect the recipient to give your resume and background while many more sit on his desk or inbox to be reviewed as well?

3. How can you be certain that there is even an actual position open? Might this posting be simply to comply with corporate HR policies…while the hiring department already has someone in mind?

4. Assuming you do get a follow-up call or e-mail from HR, how free-flowing do you feel to simply be yourself versus nervous with performance

anxiety, preparing to go under a judgmental microscope?

All of these (and more) constrictions of the standard job search approach are about to be distinguished so that you can think more deeply about what is actually going on in these everyday scenarios.

First, let's define overt versus stealth. The typical way most people search for jobs is by finding what is open that they can apply for. Whether it is a position posted on an Internet job board, company Website, or even listed with recruiters, most folks know no better than to attempt to place their square peg in a square hole in a publicly known job (advertised opening). That's overt job search: throwing your hat in the ring with every other Tom, Dick, and Harriet who saw the same posting.

An overt approach puts you in competition with everyone and limits you to only those positions that exactly match your background, because you'll only be hired if you've already done what they need done. Sorry, that's just how HR works: they want someone who already has experience doing the job before. What's worse, using an overt method is akin to wearing a sandwich board that says "I need a job!" It conveys desperation and need, which is never attractive, and is a weak place from which to enter negotiations.

CareerGuy Tip: Overt job search =
"I NEED A JOB!!!"

The Stealth Job Search Method isn't about competing with 10,000 others knocking on the door overtly, but rather proactively priming the hiring pump by simply being known and top-of-mind even before a position opens up to public knowledge. It's the job search equivalent of Wall Street insider information...except it's legal. It involves having so many seeds planted in the minds of folks far and wide that, at the exact instant any type of appropriate opportunity arises, you are thought of *first* and get the hot tip even before HR gets involved and posts the position.

 *CareerGuy Tip: Stealth job search = Wall Street insider information...but it's legal!*

The Stealth Job Search Method has you treated more like an individual, a real person, as opposed to being 1 of 10,000 beating on the door overtly. Plus, it opens up opportunities beyond what your particular background might allow because it emphasizes the power (and flexibility) of personal relationships instead of exact qualifications. We all know that people will bend rules for people they know. So, stealth search is less about desperately conveying "I need a job!" and more about using your real passions and interests to connect and stay known by people who matter.

To launch a successful stealth campaign, a simple but monumental shift in thinking and operating around your job search is necessary. You must be willing to open up a new paradigm of possibility. To demonstrate the immense power of stealth, consider a couple of examples:

> *CareerGuy Tip: Effective career shift requires paradigm shift.*

Miracle Move #1

Eileen, VP of marketing for a major telecommunications company, wanted to make a change. Possessing a limited overt-search mentality, she assumed she could only transition into another marketing role, most likely with another telecom company. At this point in her career, her values had shifted substantially. She had a passion for her Jewish culture and had always wanted to do something related to Judaism, but was accustomed to a big corporate paycheck and figured she'd have to take a deep cut—even *if* she could qualify for anything in that field. This was all before she learned The Stealth Job Search Method.

After a thorough process of career inventory and assessment, followed by personal branding and packaging, she began connecting with people under the radar, which was not about her needing a job. Rather, she began forming relationships based upon research into her true interests and passions, one of which was Judaism. She ended up landing a position as the executive director of a non-profit organization that trains bomb-sniffing dogs for Israel.

Miracle Move #2:

Jim was an entrepreneur with his own high-tech computer products manufacturing business for 25 years. Divorce rendered him out on the streets without a company. He had not put together a resume or looked for a job in 25 years. He had been holed up in his own reserved, pocket-protector engineering world for nearly his whole adult life...and didn't think he had a contact to his name.

After a morale- and self-value-building process, along with the formation and creation of a personal brand-based "research project" on the state of his high-tech industry, he began shyly meeting and greeting people using The Stealth Job Search Method. He was turned on to a local venture capital group and began creating relationships there. Trying to be of service rather than needing a job, he volunteered to scout for them, assessing opportunities that crossed their desks to provide vital feedback on the viability of their various investment opportunities. He became such a valuable asset to the group that they developed immense respect for him and chose to fund him into one of those opportunities. He went on to own 75 percent of the company.

Here are the major points to pull from these stories:

☞ Neither person would have landed these opportunities through overt means, out looking for a job like everyone else, because they weren't advertised.

☞ Neither would have reclaimed their worth without a focused, esteem-building process (career inventory) and would have come across to others just as needy as everyone else.

☞ Neither would have distinguished themselves from the masses without a personally branded approach to communicating their uniqueness.

☞ Neither would have attracted such hidden opportunities without creating wide, varied, and empowered relationships.

☞ Specifically in the case of Eileen, she would have never gotten past first base through the overt method of applying for such a role, had it even been advertised, because she didn't have that particular experience and background.

☞ Because neither was involved in standard, overt competition, they were both in a stronger position to negotiate a salary or deal.

Therein lies the beauty at the heart of The Stealth Job Search Method.

To begin to understand how it works, let's explore a bit of career wisdom often heard during job search.

80 PERCENT OF ALL JOBS ARE FILLED BEFORE THEY ARE EVER ADVERTISED

Have you heard that before? Lots of folks have, but most never dug beneath the surface to grasp its meaning or its effects on job search. Believe me, once you understand the impact of that truth, first you'll puke, then you'll change your ways. Let me walk you through a little story to demonstrate **The Evolution of a Hire.** Then, after you recover from your disgust, we will consider the implications.

In Phase 1 of The Evolution of a Hire, consider some upcoming staff changes taking place within several departments at United Amalgamated Incorporated: shipping, accounting, and marketing. In shipping, Clarisse has given notice that, for family reasons, she is moving to Lima, Ohio, within two months. In accounting, Bill isn't really cutting it as accounts payable manager, and his boss secretly wants to replace him at some point. In marketing, Gaby is considering going into business with her husband and has privately conveyed that possibility to a few close coworkers.

In each department, there are people "in the know" about the upcoming changes. In shipping, the situation is widely known because Clarisse has informed her boss and is in the process of compiling a handbook to assist her currently unknown successor. The department is even planning a going-away party for her next month, so everyone in that department knows of the future opening.

In accounting, Bill is in the dark—literally and figuratively—and his boss is keeping his concerns about Bill close to the vest. Therefore, only the boss knows of a potential opening arising there. In marketing, both the boss and most of the department are unaware of the fact that Gaby could be leaving soon. Only Gaby and her closest associates are aware of the possible slot she will leave vacant. In each case—as in most situations involving a potential job opening—there are certain folks "in the know": the whole staff, just the boss, or just the staff.

The question is this: What are the folks "in the know" doing with what they know? Take a moment just to think it through. If there is an empty desk beside you at work—or will be soon—what would *you* be doing? Telling others, right? You'd be talking to friends, family, and acquaintances about the potential opening (though sometimes discreetly, in the case of Gaby). It could casually arise in everyday conversations, or you might pointedly discuss it with folks you know who could fit the role.

CareerGuy Tip: People "in the know" talk to the people they know about openings.

You wouldn't be chatting it up just because you are a nice corporate citizen or want to help others, though those may be partly true. Maybe you get a referral bonus from HR, and you could pocket some money from it. Though the bigger reason is not related to money, it's completely and similarly selfish: you care about your workplace—specifically your department—and you want it to be the most enjoyable and productive environment possible. Because you spend most of your waking hours at work, you have a vested interest in *who* you interact with in your everyday activities. You would obviously rather have a known, competent entity sitting at the desk beside you than risk Human Resources sending in some unknown bozo you have to risk getting along with. That's why the people "in the know" talk to the people they know.

CareerGuy Tip: People have a vested interest in who they work with.

As an outsider looking for a job, however, what if you are not known by someone "in the know"? Take Jane or Joe Jobseeker, for instance. If Jane or Joe approaches the company for work, they will most likely interact with Human Resources. Because HR is not yet privy to the in-the-know information about the future openings (remember, at this point, it's only known by the people in that department), they merely add Jane and Joe's resumes to the thousands already in the database. "We'll keep you in mind for the future" is the most attention Jane or Joe Jobseeker gets.

But, to reiterate, those in the know are referring the people they know into the department. Those folks come in, have casual conversations with the manager—"Oh, you're Tony's friend. Sure, grab a cup of coffee, let's sit down and talk"—and many get hired.

Think about it: the manager has a personal referral of this person from Tony. Tony has stuck his neck out to attest to this person's value. That's always going to carry more weight than some unknown person HR might come up with later. That's not because Tony is better than HR, but because Tony may have a closer understanding of the position and the hiring manager can more likely beat up on Tony later if it doesn't work out. Remember, at this point, HR doesn't know about the opening and therefore isn't helping to fill it, yet the manager has one of her current employees putting his own reputation on the line to refer someone. That carries weight.

This process continues through Phase 2 of The Evolution of a Hire, during which knowledge of the potential opening—if it has not been filled in Phase 1—has grown wider. Perhaps there is now a concerted effort to put together a formal hiring requisition for HR. How long can that take? In some large, bureaucratic organizations, it can take weeks or months. But right now, today, Jane or Joe Jobseeker runs into the same database wall if they approach the company for a job overtly: HR still doesn't officially know about the opening, so they can only take a resume for the database.

All the while, through friendly referral conversations within the department, folks are still coming in, chatting with the boss, and some are getting jobs. Of course, HR will eventually have to get involved and rubber stamp those coming in via stealth means with their official employee badge, but those savvy, stealth folks made the most important contact *first*—with the hiring manager! They focused on running into people, not a database.

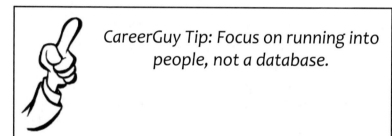

CareerGuy Tip: Focus on running into people, not a database.

By the end of Phase 2 in The Evolution of a Hire, many jobs have been filled by friendly referrals. Lots of casual conversations have taken place between the hiring managers and friends, relatives, or acquaintances of the people in the know. The managers have developed a comfort level because, through that referral, they sense that they know more about these prospective employees than if they just came off the street. Someone has vouched for the newbie…and the manager knows where that vouching person works and lives.

Consider this: If you need a babysitter, lawyer, or tax accountant, don't you feel more safe talking to those your friends refer you to *first*, rather than simply opening up the yellow pages? The more known an entity is—or at least seems—the higher the comfort level that exists in doing business with that person. **This is why 80 percent of all jobs are filled before they are ever advertised.**

But let's not leave it there. There's more gut-wrenching required to fully purge the old mindset and start afresh. Let's discuss what happens in Phase 3 of The Evolution of a Hire.

Imagine, for some strange reason, that after all of these stealth conversations have taken place, those jobs remain open...and HR is now in possession of the requisition. Working diligently, they list the openings on the company Website, post them on various job boards, and maybe even farm them out to a few headhunters. What do you think then happens to HR? Can you say, *inundated?*

HR then receives thousands of resumes for every position they want to fill! Their challenge is to find the needle in a haystack: the most qualified and perfect fit for that role. If you are Jane or Joe Jobseeker—one of the thousands applying overtly—what is your competitive stance? Zilch. How about your negotiating power? Nada.

It reminds me of a scene from the 1940 film, *The Grapes of Wrath*, when Henry Fonda balked at the boss man sitting behind the hiring table, asking him, "Okay, mister. What you paying?"

"Two and a half cents," he replied.

"Two and a half? Say, mister, a man can't make his dinner on that."

"Take it or leave it. There are men coming in from the South will be glad to get it."

"But how are we gonna eat?"

"Look…I didn't set the price. If you want it, Okay. If you don't, turn around and beat it."

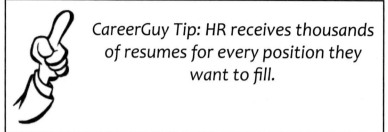

CareerGuy Tip: HR receives thousands of resumes for every position they want to fill.

Applying overtly, you *start out* with absolutely no competitive stance or negotiating power. Besides that, consider the interview environment you'll step into *if* you're one of the 20 or so resumes that get parceled through for a first-cut, pre-screen phone interview. Is this a friendly and loving environment? Are these HR folks ready and willing to support you in your dreams and aspirations, compassionate and understanding of the fact that none of us are perfect and yet we all have unique and valuable talents to express? Will they be able to see you for who you really are and what you can become beneath or beyond your past titles, salaries, employment gaps, or skill shortcomings?

HR professionals have an incredibly tough task: to whittle down thousands of resumes to one single person. Therefore, your interactions will not occur in a truly friendly environment, but a rather hostile one. Don't get me wrong, HR folks are nice, and will be nice to you. That's the whole reason they went into HR—because they like people. But the challenging demands of their job ensure that they can never really bond with potential hires beyond the facts, and, first and foremost, they have to get their jobs done.

Therefore, as Jane or Joe Jobseeker responding overtly to an ad, you will have adversarial interviews. Not blatantly, mind you, but underneath the pleasantries, in the mindset, the critic will be lurking. HR is looking for why you are NOT right for this job! They want to find the kinks in your armor— where and how you might be lying! They have to whittle the slate down, and you are just as apt a target as the next applicant. Now that's a great energy to engage with, right?

Lastly, given what we've learned about what the people in the know do when they know about an opening, realize this: Any position publicly known through an ad, headhunter, or site posting has likely already been "touched" by *lots* of people. Folks have come in stealth and discussed it with the boss, rummaged over it, parceled through it, and so on. Yet, it's still open!

What might that say about the position? Answer: It may not be a plum role. That's not to say all advertised positions are worthless, but you have to realize that a *lot* of people already knew about it before it was advertised.

So, let's add up what you get through responding to an ad:

☞ Zero competitive stance.

☞ Zero negotiating power.

☞ Adversarial interviews.

☞ All for what is probably not a plum position.

The Evolution of a Hire

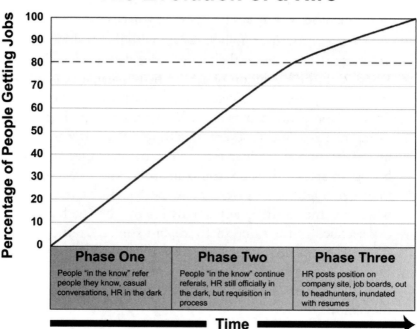

Concept adapted from the work of the late J. Michael Farr, *The Very Quick Job Search*, 1st Ed, JISTWorks.

Awakening to this, why would someone *ever* pursue job search overtly, applying for jobs like everyone else? Doing so is openly declaring that you will accept the dregs of the job world, the scraps of career leftovers thrown out into the alleyways of scrounging, vocational varmints. You're worth more than that!

Here's my acronym for the word "Apply":

Absence of

People

Power

Leveraging

Your career

If you're not known by the people in the know, you're basically without any power or leverage to differentiate yourself from the other lemmings being overtly needy.

Compare this overt folly, however, with the stealth bonanza. Those who came on the scene under the radar in Phases 1 and 2 of The Evolution of a Hire had casual, easy conversations. They weren't subjected to a competitive environment. Though competition may have been present—perhaps the hiring manager meets several stealth referrals—it wasn't deliberately rubbed in their faces. Plus, because they met the hiring manager through someone they knew, the hiring manager might have given them the benefit of the doubt when it came to the qualifications for the job (perhaps not experienced in the same software, but similar), rather than the weed-them-out/adversarial nature of typical HR meetings. For sure, even a stealth referral has to meet the basic requirements...but we all know people bend the rules for people they know.

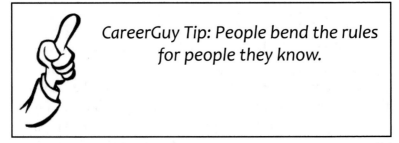

CareerGuy Tip: People bend the rules for people they know.

In truth, we should add a preliminary phase to our model here—a "Before the Opening" phase—which even precedes anyone's awareness of a job coming up. It was in this "Before the Opening" phase where the stage was set and the seeds planted. Prior to word getting out that Clarisse was moving, Joe was going to be replaced, or Gaby would be resigning to start her own business, there were just people getting to know other people in the course of everyday life. This "getting to know, and be known by" people paid off when the openings arose.

In other words, you don't just want to talk to people in companies where there is a current opening, and you also don't want to wait around until you are unemployed before making those connections. Rather, you want to connect with people far and wide, even if there's no job available for the moment, all the time and everywhere...because one day you'll need another opportunity and one day there will be one available where there isn't one now.

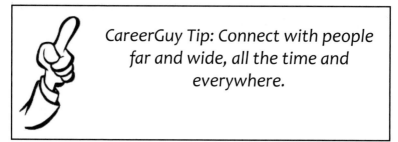

CareerGuy Tip: Connect with people far and wide, all the time and everywhere.

Best-selling author and astute businessman Harvey Mackay wrote a book called *Dig Your Well Before You're Thirsty.* That title says it all! The time to drill down and tap into the infinite resources of connections and relationships is *before* you need them, and anyone can tap that source of goodwill if you learn how to drill effectively.

There are at least three ways to utilize this method in your career. First, you might want to learn how to conduct a job-search-focused stealth campaign when you are unemployed. Second, perhaps you want to utilize an opportunity-focused stealth campaign when you are considering an entrepreneurial venture. Third, it would be smart to simply employ and manage a career-maintenance-focused stealth campaign at all times (even when you are currently employed or engaged). In every case, you set yourself up to always be known by the people "in the know"…and to reap the benefits of that exposure.

That's just how the stealth door swings. Your only mission in a stealth approach to job search or career management is to get known and stay known by people "in the know." Jobs, opportunities, projects, and involvements will take care of themselves. Whether you want a job, to build your own business and client base, or even to find a mate or partner, effective relationship building is required…and getting in by stealth means is the basis for uncovering the best opportunities in any economy.

Chapter 3: The 4M Method of Career Management

Before we dive into the 10 Time-Tested Principles for Launching an Effective Stealth Campaign, let's establish an overall context for these principles and a way to view the consistent, long-term building of a career tribe. The objective, as we have discussed, is to know and be known.

There are 4 pillars upon which your campaign should be built, which I call the **4M Method of Career Management**:

Meet people, in a

Memorable way, so as to stay top-of-

Mind, and then

Maintain those relationships for life.

MEET

The first M is evident: you have to meet people. *Anywhere and everywhere.* That means not just somebody in a suit in an office, but also someone in swimming trunks beside you on the beach. It means not just someone you're walking with through an office lobby door, but also the doorman himself!

But what is the reason people don't freely converse with those around them throughout the day? Mostly because of one common hindrance: fear.

FEAR BLOCKS OUR UNIVERSAL GOODIES

There are people all around you all day long. You don't know who those people are, and more importantly, you don't know who they know! Yet, even with the wellspring of potential connections for information and referrals surrounding us, most people are prevented from capitalizing on it based on fear.

I have a personal belief that whatever it is that you are seeking is actually seeking you! But guess what. You have to get out there and initiate some conversations so that the goodies the universe has in store for you can make their way over!

CareerGuy Tip: What you are seeking is seeking you, but you have to say, "Hello! I'm here!"

Want to do a quick and profound check on how the universe is lining up your world to give you what you need? This exercise should be allotted an hour or so. Go to your local coffee house, grab your favorite beverage, and sit at a table. Don't read anything, don't text or check e-mails, and don't even have your PDA or computer out on the table. Just sit there, observing. Watch people, with a slight smile on your face. Don't be in a rush to do anything or get anywhere, and don't have any busy work out at all.

After you've sat for a few minutes, just watching, no doubt, someone will start talking to you. Just try it! If nobody does, turn to another person sitting nearby, and say something such as, "Wonderful day, isn't it?" Find some easygoing reason to get into a conversation with someone. If the first person doesn't budge, no problem. Just sit for a bit more, happy-go-lucky, and find someone else to start a conversation with. Then find out about that person, what he does, what she's up to, and make some mental notes of what comes out of the conversation.

What you may notice is that very often, the universe puts folks around us that either have information we can use, or we have information they can use. In many ways, the universe is conspiring for our highest and greatest good, but we are unaware of that fact because we tend to stay secluded, private, and afraid in our own little world.

CareerGuy Tip: The universe puts folks around us who have information we can use, or we have information they can use.

We all have an unsubstantiated, underlying fear of each other which makes us stay to ourselves. All the old voices ingrained within us still tell us, "Don't talk to strangers," "Don't bother people," and "Mind your own business."

Do you believe people like interacting with one another? Do you believe that people like helping one another? When I ask these questions at live events, the majority of hands go up. Yes, underneath it all, we believe that people like to interact and even help one another when they can. Yet, we play it so safe out in the world, reticent to simply meet and greet and see what treat the universe has in store for us.

The reason: rejection. As unwarranted as it may be in our adult states, we still operate as though someone out there won't like us, won't approve of us, or may hurt us. Those are childish fears and, as the acronym reminds us, False Evidence Appearing Real.

I'm not saying to go hang out on the streets and back alleys and talk to every soul that walks by, but that extreme is a far cry from the simple willingness to start up a conversation with the person in front or behind you in the line at the grocery store. The fact is, you have no idea who is around you!

That person behind you in line might just be the brother-in-law of your next employer. That person sitting beside you in the dentist's office might just be your next client. What does it hurt to find some harmless way to start up a conversation and find out what the people around you do? The funny thing is, when you ask someone what he does, he will generally also ask what you do. It's good to always have a business card to give, and to request a card, at such meetings. You never know how and when you may want to reconnect.

CareerGuy Tip: You have no idea who is around you. Check in, and reap the rewards.

At a recent business forum, a friend and I were standing in the foyer before entering the auditorium where a major CEO would be interviewed as part of a public launch of his book. My friend and I looked around and were shocked to notice that, while everyone waited in the foyer, 90 percent of the people who weren't in a conversation with someone were head-down *glued* to their PDAs! Texts were flying off fingers, e-mails were being answered, and the Web was being surfed...but *people weren't talking to one another!* If the universe is sprinkling our surroundings with people we have information for or vice versa, why do we cheat ourselves of the opportunity to get it?

When I lead seminars for folks who've been recently laid off, I send the participants out to lunch with a few simple instructions: Go out and create a few conversations with people you don't know. Of course, I've had to talk long and hard with them beforehand about the necessity of getting outside of their comfort zones in order to create different results for themselves. One thing is for sure: if you're going to have different (that is, stealth) results, then you have to think differently and do things differently.

People have created some phenomenal results by playing the game of meet, greet, and find the treat. Here are some examples:

The information technology professional who scoped out the food court and saw someone sitting at a table alone. He casually asked if he could sit across, and did so. After eating for a bit in silence while the other person read the paper, he initiated a conversation about the food, which gradually led to discussing the companies in the surrounding area, which led to him finding out that the person he sat beside was the IT manager of a Fortune 500 insurance company just up the street. They had a long talk about technology and industry trends and became generally acquainted. The conversation ended with my seminar participant being asked to send over his resume and a plan to talk further. This all occurred for a 50ish-year-old man who had left for lunch *terrified* that his assignment was to go talk to people he didn't know! But, kudos to him, because he was coachable, and more committed to new results in his life than the comfort zone he had gotten used to. Subsequently, I heard that he made a point of going out to the food court in the mall in his hometown a few times a week, simply because of the success he seemed to have there. It had nothing to do with the food court, and everything to do with him being brave enough to just try it!

The accountant who took my coaching to not discount anyone and spoke to the doorman during our lunch break. She spoke to him about his job and how much he liked what he did. She asked him how much he knew about the different companies in the building and, after describing what she did, found out from him about an entertainment business management firm in the building. She passed by their office on her way back to the seminar, spoke to them briefly and was given the card of someone to follow up with later in the week. Maybe she could have just found out about that firm by looking on the building directory...but she hadn't!

And, had she not spoken to the doorman—who knew of every company in the building—she wouldn't have had a lead to follow up with the next week.

The research scientist who, knowing that his homework was to create some conversations with people he didn't know, actually decided to chat with a neighbor that he had always seen in his garage every evening...someone he had passed by and casually waved to for months. Turns out, the guy had a hobby of crafting custom furniture in his garage. My participant, who had confessed in the seminar of loving to do things with his hands, found it intriguing and they decided to work on some projects together. And, it just so happened to also come up in conversation that the man in the garage was the CEO of a solar cell company and was interested in seeing the background of my participant, given his company was in a heavy research mode.

 *CareerGuy Tip: Social Media Fair Use Clause—Don't let the world of high-tech negate the value of high-touch.*

These are just a few of hundreds of stories of how people create new possibilities for themselves by getting beyond their fears of simply connecting with the people around them... and these stories only highlight the *professional* goodies. Believe me, for *anything* you want in life—be it a new job, a new client, a new relationship, a new hobby partner—talking to people is always the answer. Of course, you can talk to people

on a massive scale these days with social
media…but don't let the world of high-tech
negate or discount the value of high-touch.
Meet, greet, and find the treat!

So far, we've only discussed the folks around you in everyday life. What about the people you "already know?" I
put that in quotations because, I dare say, you only *think* you
know the people in your life. If you had a different method,
perhaps outside of the standard way of relating to them as
you do now, you may find out that the people right under
your nose have information, knowledge, and contacts that
you've never even imagined.

And what about the people you don't know well yet, but
whom you know *of*? What about that person you've only seen
or heard of who is in a field that you've always been interested in exploring? What about the speaker who addressed
your community or trade group about a particular topic of
interest to you? What about the owner of the shop down the
street who is selling a line that intrigues you? What about the
parent of your child's schoolmate whom you heard has a home-
based business that sounds fascinating?

There are folks to talk to about careers and interests *anywhere and everywhere!* There's even the chief marketing officer or senior research scientist of SuperBig Conglomerate as
well—folks you don't have any connection to whatsoever and
yet, with the proper methods, you could even get to know
them and have them know you. The world is your oyster in
terms of having folks to talk to! All you need is a savvy approach…to get in with them, and to get in **good** with them.

MEMORABLE

To begin with, if you only started practicing meeting people in front of or behind you in the checkout line, you'd see how memorable that is to them! The sad truth is, most people don't stick their neck out to meet, greet, and find the treat in those around them...so your doing so is already memorable. But beyond the "random acts of find-ness" that you can conduct every day, how do you make yourself memorable, say, to the chief marketing officer of SuperBig Conglomerate, when she doesn't know you from Adam?

CareerGuy Tip: Conduct random acts of find-ness, finding the info exchange treat in everyone around you.

It certainly isn't by telling them you need a job! That's easily forgettable. Matter of fact, they actually won't even pay it any mind. To be memorable, you have to do something other than what the masses do. Your approach must be one of earnest and sincere interest in something of interest to them, and it must be cultivated and conducted out of that interest alone...with no ulterior motives. (It doesn't hurt to have in place some personal branding, which I'm a big advocate of...but that's another book.)

Coupled with a meticulously managed follow-up system, a memorable approach can open doors to information, relationships, mentorship and, yes, even opportunities for employment or engagement that would never happen if you were out in a me-me-me mode as many others are. Me-me-me isn't memorable—but your interest in another person is.

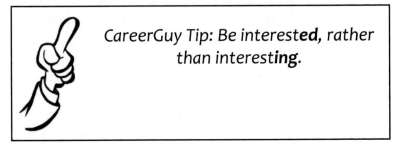

CareerGuy Tip: Be interest**ed**, rather than interest**ing**.

MIND (TOP-OF, THAT IS)

Your ability to gain knowledge, to create relationships, to open doors, and to step into new, exciting, and ever-more-perfect career opportunities for yourself will come from one place: the top-of-mind awareness of the people who need to know *you* for *you* to get where *you* want to go.

Phases 1 and 2 of The Evolution of a Hire prove the point. How could you be known by those "in the know" unless you were somehow located in their short-term random access memory? Therefore, your job is to both climb to top-of-mind status and to stay top-of-mind by going far beyond simple one-off meetings and idle coffee-line conversations by *creating ongoing relationships.* When you have relationships far and wide, your reach becomes far and wide.

Simple analogy: what if you were a radio station nestled in a valley with a mountain ridge surrounding you on all sides? Could people hear your broadcast in the valley? Sure. Could listeners call in to make song requests? You bet. But can they hear you on the other side of that mountain ridge? Nope!

But, if you get smart, you might decide to strategically place several antennae atop that mountain ridge. Can they hear your broadcasts on the other side of the mountain ridge now? Yes they can. Can those listeners call in with their song requests? Absolutely.

Setting up antennae is a smart move, and keeps broadcasting radio waves of awareness of who you are to the world. That's what I call establishing your career tribe: the folks you want to know you, and whom you want operating as your antennae in the world.

MAINTAIN

The problem with mechanical things such as antennae is that they get worn and rusty when the elements beat on them, and they start to fall apart due to lack of maintenance. That's why it's critical to maintain those career tribe relationships *even when you're in the throes of your current position!*

Most folks think of their antennae only when they are face-to-face with urgent need. It's all too common, once landing, to submerge into the new company, new job, or new responsibilities and let those antennae go untended and neglected. Of course, you need to give your best wherever you land, but if you can take on the mindset that you need to keep a percentage of your attention reserved for the inevitable "down the road" that will someday occur, there's always the capacity to do the necessary rounds of maintenance to keep those antennae buzzing.

If a concerned doctor asked whether you'd rather exercise one hour a day or die in the next month, which would you choose? Of course you would exercise. You'd find the time. The same applies to your career. Which fits your busy schedule better, staying in contact with your career tribe on a regular and ongoing basis to stay abreast of news and opportunities that can move you and your career forward? Or being out of work for months and beginning yet another networking campaign from scratch?

An old oil filter commercial used to show a mechanic discussing how to best maintain a car to avoid costly major repairs. His advice was, "You can pay me now...or you can pay me later." Depending on the analogy that works best, you can call it either maintaining your career fitness or your career mobility by continually investing time and resources on a steady and ongoing basis into your capacity to make a career move on short notice.

 *CareerGuy Tip: Build up your career fitness muscles and career mobility assurance by investing in maintaining your career tribe.*

Here's something to think about: Might there be lots of other opportunities coming up that it would pay for you to know about even though you're currently situated in one? You bet. From the point of view that you own your own busy-ness, and therefore need to make sure you're getting the highest return for your assets, it's smart business to know what the market is presenting in terms of investment opportunities.

Just like physical health, though many people don't "make time" in their schedule for exercise until they know how critically important it is, you'll never know for sure how critical it is for your career to keep the tribe alive until you need it. Is ignorance really all that blissful?

With The 4M Method of Career Transition now providing a contextual foundation for our path, let's look into the actual philosophy and practice of **10 Time-Tested Principles for Launching an Effective Stealth Campaign** to land you your next opportunity, and the next, and the next, and...

PART 2:

10 Time-Tested Principles for Launching an Effective Stealth Campaign

Principle # 1: The Best Way to Get a Job Is: Don't Be Looking for One

In a *stealth approach* to career management, your *only* task is to *meet* and *be known by* as many people as possible. It is *not* to look for a job.

Let that sink in a bit. I know it sounds crazy, but you really need to begin to crack open that traditional, overt-search mindset. Look, anyone can do a typical job search. That doesn't require any particular savvy. But think about it: you grabbed this book so that you could do something different than the rest!

 CareerGuy Tip: Desperation works in job search as well as it does in dating.

Have you ever noticed that desperation doesn't sell well in life? Whether you're looking for a mate or a job, needy people are not that attractive...and can even be repellant. In the long run, being out on the road knocking on doors because you need a job will have you meet, get to know, and be known by fewer people than by using the stealth method. They'll either have a job for you or they won't, and off you go, never to connect with them again. Therefore, I say, the best way to get a job is to *not* be looking for one.

 **CareerGuy Tip: Your only task in stealth career management is to know and be known by people.**

Notice that I didn't say: Don't be out there meeting people. Given The 4M Method of Career Management, you absolutely *must* be meeting people left and right. However, you'll meet—get to know and be known by—many more people when you meet them *for reasons outside of your need for a job.*

Let's talk a bit about human nature. Do you believe human beings enjoy helping one another? I do. But, I believe people also have a primary objective in life that can sometimes get in the way of helping others: to win. Everyone wants to win. Nobody wants to lose. As human beings, we naturally avoid situations in which we might lose and gravitate towards those where we stand the best chance of winning.

People want to win in their careers. People want to win in their relationships. People want to win in their health and fitness. People want to win in their finances. People want to win in bringing their goals and desires to pass. We all seek to win, and that doesn't mean anyone else has to lose necessarily...we just want to come out a winner.

Applied to the job search, when you attempt to meet people because you need a job, you'll generally meet fewer folks because they will avoid a situation in which they might lose. What if they don't know of any jobs? What if they don't really understand what you do, your field, or what you're looking for? Of course, there are always the try-to-be-helpful-anyway types...but on average, people will shy away from a situation in which they don't know the score, and face the potential of looking bad. Plus, people vehemently avoid being put in a position of having to say no. Do you like saying no to people? Nobody does.

So, paradoxically, in your quest for a new position, you must actually find reasons to meet people *other than your need for a job*. Many folks have heard the term "informational interviews." It refers to the idea of gaining information from people through interviewing them on a particular profession, industry, or career path. It is designed to allow the job-seeker to try out a job (at least mentally, by what she can find out about it) before she tries to actually get the job. However, more often than not, it is used as only a thinly veiled attempt to actually get hired.

 *CareerGuy Tip: In a job search, find reasons to meet people other than your need for a job.*

Though the concept has been around for 40 years or so, informational interviewing is still better than the standard, overt "Can I have a job?" approach that most people live by. But the traditional practice of informational interviewing requires a dramatic overhaul to be a truly effective tool for career management. To ask for an "informational interview" today has become cliché, as most people recognize this as a disguised attempt to get a job. And remember, if they think you are looking for a job, fewer folks will meet with you...no matter how you mask it.

Therefore, the approach I advocate is to forget looking for a job altogether. As counter-intuitive as it may be, just drop it! You're going to come out way ahead if you do. And, instead of looking for a job, I suggest adopting Principle #2.

Principle # 2: An Ounce of Research Is Worth a Pound of Job Search

Don't think I'm putting a new face on an old concept. There is a stark difference from the decrepit practice of "informational interviews" and what I'll propose here...and can be best introduced through a true story.

A client of mine had a long and impressive career in marketing for various high-tech companies, most recently a major-brand printer manufacturer. However, due to reorganization, he was laid off and had spent the last year consulting with a couple of partners. Their standard approach was to contact CEOs to attempt to set up meetings in which they would inquire as to the challenges the company was facing.

Of course, if they could isolate issues, they could then pitch a proposal to the CEO to solve those issues as outside consultants to the company. Out of 100 initial calls they would make to CEOs—to try to arrange these meetings—perhaps 10 calls were returned. This left my client and his partners with few opportunities to pitch their services and get to know and be known by these CEOs.

If you look at their approach, it's easy to see the principle I've described in action. When they made their initial calls, to discover the pain of the CEO so that they could be the healer, it was apparent that they were looking for a job. Consulting, temporary employment, permanent employment—the same rule applies: if people know you're looking for a job, you'll meet fewer people. Again, not because they're mean… but because they don't want to be put in the position of having to say no or being unable to help. Therefore, only a small percentage of their calls were returned. Their outreach had "We need a job!" written all over it.

CareerGuy Tip: In all areas of life, people avoid situations in which they might have to say no.

However, upon grasping Principle #2: An Ounce of Research is Worth a Pound of Job Search, my client informed his partners that they would begin to approach these CEOs differently. They decided to write articles for high-tech magazines focusing on the electronic products that he and his partners consulted on. From that point forward, all outreach calls were only to request appointments with CEOs to interview them for articles.

Immediately, the returned-call response rate shot up from 10 percent to 90 percent. And, true to their word—you can't fake actually *doing* research—they would go in, interview the CEOs, and write articles based on those interviews. Yet, what inevitably occurred after the interview was that the CEO would want to know more about my client and his partners, why they were doing this research, and more about their services. It opened the door for describing themselves as "thought leaders" in the field, at the cutting edge of development, and resulted in many more consulting gigs than they ever obtained through cold calling for a job.

The point that my client proved so well was that *finding a reason other than your need for a job* to connect with people will always get you farther. But you have to be genuine about it. Trying to fake it that you are researching when you really just want a job is seen through immediately. That's why I teach clients to set up research projects around things they are truly fascinated by and passionate about.

If there is something at the cutting edge of your industry, say a new technique that is being employed in your profession, or a trend that is affecting the industry, *something that authentically interests you*, then that is a subject ripe for a research project.

CareerGuy Tip: What you're truly interested in or passionate about is worthy of a research project.

For example, one of my career transition clients produced the live-action thrill shows at theme parks, where you sit and watch mock-ups of major hit movie themes, with high-adventure stunts, good guys, bad guys, and so on. He had designed these productions for years, but was out of work. I asked if he really loved what he did, which he emphatically affirmed. I then asked what was at the cutting edge of the industry and what was it that still interested him in the field. He said that he had always wondered why these live shows couldn't have an audience-participation element affecting the turn of events, such as each audience member having a hand-held controller to input their choices or opinions that would then influence the outcome of the show.

I told him that this sounded like an excellent subject for a research project! His going in to meet with players in that world based on a question such as that was a far cry from someone simply hoofing it for a job. If you look hard, you might even see a bit of a mission or vision involved here... which is far more attractive than need.

Research projects may also focus on areas completely outside of what you have traditionally done for work, subjects you might generally classify as only interests or hobbies. The amazing truth I've seen played out many times is that, when someone researches a subject that he is genuinely passionate about, even if only currently a hobby, through getting to know and be known by people, he will often make inroads into that field work-wise and end up changing careers completely!

Here is another example to help drive this home. Remember Eileen from the Miracle Move #1 example earlier? She came to me when she was the VP of marketing for a large telecommunications company. Eileen wanted out of that situation for various reasons, and thought her only option was to transition into another marketing role with another telecommunications company. That is the myopic perspective most folks have in career transition because traditional thinking says, "Someone will only hire me to do exactly what I've done before." In overt search, it's absolutely true. In a stealth approach, it's malleable.

> **CareerGuy Tip: In overt search, you're limited to what you've done before. Using a stealth approach, you have leeway to make new choices.**

What she was genuinely passionate about was neither cutting-edge marketing concepts nor the field of telecommunication, but her Jewish culture and faith. Earlier in her career, she had served a stint in marketing at the local Jewish Federation, but had found non-profit compensation lagging behind traditional corporate pay. She had always wanted to be more involved in the Jewish culture and had only dreamed of somehow working somewhere that could compensate her adequately.

The standard, overt approach would have seen her pursuing other telecom companies to do the same thing she had done before. But, I coached her in the stealth mindset. After some extensive career inventory and personal branding work—to distinguish her unique essence beyond titles and employers, and therefore become memorable—she took on a research project to explore the state of the Jewish culture and met people far and wide outside of her small, telecommunications niche.

Through relationships that she developed during that research, she was referred to more people than she would have ever met outside of such a research project. People started getting to know her, and to see her skills and talents outside of the strict definition of "marketing" and "telecom." One person led to another person, one bit of information or advice led to another, and eventually someone simply mentioned to her that he knew someone looking for a particular person and how Eileen really fit the bill. The result was that she became the executive director of a non-profit organization that trains bomb-sniffing dogs for Israel!

Did she get that role because she had any experience as a non-profit executive director? Not at all. However, through simply meeting and getting known by people far and wide in her field of passionate interest, at some point someone said, "You know, given who you are and what you're capable of (outside of your titles and background), you'd probably be good for this role I heard about." It was *finding a reason other than her need for a job* that led her to meet more people, got her on the radar of folks with connections, and opened up this opportunity for her.

All of these clients demonstrated that, when you remove the desperation and single-eyed focus of "I need a job!" from your interactions and explorations, doors open and you elicit assistance and opportunities that would not have come otherwise.

In the next section, we will explore the creation of research projects for your own stealth campaign, similarly based in what you're truly passionate about. By authentically researching your interests rather than needy job hunting, you begin to attract rather than repel the relationships and situations that truly interest you.

CareerGuy Tip: Being interested attracts. Being needy repels.

But, before moving on to our next principle, first a word from our sponsor: Your Higher Calling! In order to adequately cover Principle #3, I will have to climb back onto the soapbox for a bit.

Your Higher Calling

The fear and uncertainty of the unknown too often shapes the mood of a career transition, which has folks lose out on the blessing of the shift. I believe transitions occur for a reason beyond what we can understand in the moment, yet are definitely directed and guided. I once heard a minister say, "Never waste the opportunity of a good crisis!" What he went on to explain was that, what we often perceive initially as a negative event actually has the seeds within it of a greater overall direction for our lives.

 *CareerGuy Tip: Never waste the opportunity of a good crisis.*

Face it: None of us like change. Left to our own devices, the majority of us would just keep doing what we're doing—regardless of our lack of enthusiasm, joy, challenge, or even fair compensation for it. I believe a career transition comes as a wake-up call for us to redirect our efforts in ways that fit who we have become since our last transition.

Throughout time, our skills, interests, and values evolve. Often, people don't recognize or address their evolution. They merely make do with things as they are, suck it up, and sell out on themselves. That's why Thoreau said most people live "lives of quiet desperation."

As uncertain as the unknown may be, a transition is an opportunity to reassess, recalibrate, and reengage in a work-life worth living. In the throes of the "busy-ness" of your last role, you didn't have time to adequately recognize or inventory your evolved skills, interests, or values. Therefore, a transition can be a wonderful opportunity to take stock, just like any business does on a regular basis. Conducting an insightful "career inventory" can net you many surprises to be capitalized upon in an effective stealth campaign.

CareerGuy Tip: A career transition is simply an opportunity to take stock of yourself, your assets, your interests, and your direction.

Many folks are well aware that they are spent in their current job, but live under the maxim that "the devil you know is better than the one you don't." So they stay in a dead-end job. I think that is a sad way to rationalize the wholesale forfeiture of self-expression in one's work, where you spend one-third to half of your waking hours!

The biggest fear in a career transition is simply the unknown of what's out there…but I personally believe we live in an upwardly spiraling universe where "the best is yet to come" is more than just a verse from a Sinatra tune. It takes stepping forward with faith—even in the face of the unknown—to find that greater expression of yourself.

If you saw the third Indiana Jones movie, *The Last Crusade*, you remember that Indy's second challenge was to cross a gorge to get to the Holy Grail. With no bridge in sight, it seemed impossible, and therefore called upon a "leap of faith." He had to put his foot out into the cavernous ravine to, supposedly, walk to the other side. It required all of the courage and fortitude he had within him, but he did it… and discovered that there was, in fact, an invisible bridge underneath his feet that simply blended into the cliff itself— unseen, but there nonetheless.

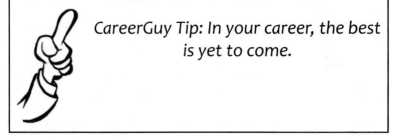

CareerGuy Tip: In your career, the best is yet to come.

Have you ever had something supposedly "bad" happen to you in life that, in retrospect, you now see as being perfect? Perhaps it was a doorway to another direction you pursued. Maybe it opened you up for something you wouldn't have been available for otherwise. It may have brought with it a multitude of unexpected benefits you could never have planned for.

Come on, let's take just a minute to look...so this isn't just theoretical. Grab your Career Transformation Insights Journal and write out your answers to just a few simple questions.

Bad or Good: You Choose

1. What are some turning point "bad" events that have occurred in your life?

   Did you ever get fired from a job?

   Did your business close down?

   Did a relationship end?

   Did you lose money on an investment?

   What was a "bad" turning point unique to you, if none of these apply?

2. If I were to pay you $1,000 for each possible "good" result that you could say came out of that "bad" occurrence, what could you come up with?

How did you being freed up from that job help you see or hear the next opportunity for you? Could you have seen or heard it when you were so busy in the other role?

How did starting over, after the closing down of your business, give you a new lease on life or offer you a new direction you would not have had if you were still tied to that business?

How did moving beyond that past relationship allow you to see yourself and what you want for yourself better than you had before?

How did the loss of the money bring about more appreciation for your life or new activities that wouldn't have happened before? What did you *gain* for the loss?

What potential "good" actually came out of your own uniquely "bad" turning point?

Even if being laid off was the reason you picked up this book, it might not be a bad thing. I've been present at termination notices when the affected persons, after being notified by their manager or HR and then brought to see me, actually waited until the HR person left the room and did a victory dance saying, "*Yes! Yes! Yes!*" They had wanted to be out of that situation for a while, but just hadn't exercised the courage to do it themselves. But even for those who weren't necessarily so elated, in talking with them, I would often hear that they had secretly wanted to move on for a while.

If we look past our immediate, breast-beating victim-hood on certain events in our life, it's possible to see that things happen for a reason. Perhaps your hidden prayers were actually answered with that layoff? Maybe you were truly feeling the yoke of that business and it was constraining your new desires for self-expression? Possibly it was just time to let that relationship go so that the right person could finally show up...now that you had done your homework on finding out what you *didn't* want? And what if you just needed to take life a little more preciously sweet and that lost investment was your wake-up call?

> ## "Do not judge, and you will never be mistaken."
> ### ~Jean Jaques Rousseau

It really all comes down to what you're going to say about whatever happened. Shakespeare said, "There is nothing good or bad, but thinking makes it so." As hard as it may seem, if I really did give you that $1,000 per "good" reason, I guarantee you'd come up with some. And often, it really isn't hard at all...if you just think differently.

If you can see that there are bad events in your life that can be retroactively seen as good, know that you don't have to wait until the event is in the long distant past to convert it. Jump on it proactively! I invite you to *look forward* from that perspective now. Take each step forward in your own leap of faith, accepting that you *know* that the unknown has hidden and wonderful surprises in store for you.

Everything in life holds both a blessing and a curse. We deny this when we label the events of our lives as either good or bad. The following old Zen story illustrates this lesson most effectively.

A farmer had a horse, but one day the horse ran away, and so the farmer and his son had to plow their fields themselves. Their neighbors said, "Oh, what bad luck that your horse ran away!" But the farmer replied, "Bad luck, good luck, who knows?"

The next week, the horse returned to the farm, bringing a herd of wild horses with him. "What wonderful luck!" cried the neighbors, but the farmer responded, "Good luck, bad luck, who knows?"

Then, the farmer's son was thrown as he tried to ride one of the wild horses, and he broke his leg. "Ah, such bad luck," sympathized the neighbors. Once again, the farmer responded, "Bad luck, good luck, who knows?"

A short time later, the ruler of the country recruited all young men to join his army for battle. The son, with his broken leg, was left at home. "What good luck that your son was not forced into battle!" celebrated the neighbors. And the farmer remarked, "Good luck, bad luck, who knows?"

Principle #3: A Question-Able Person Creates Enthusiastic Relationships

The opportunity that lies before you, if you make the mental shifts called for in Principles 1 and 2, is that of a kid in a candy store: You now get to go play in whatever playgrounds you choose!

Face it, to go out and interview for a job similar to the one you grew tired of five years ago will be difficult at best. I'm not saying getting your bills paid isn't important, but I encourage you to not waste the opportunity of a good crisis—the chance to explore those fields, interests, and dreams that you've put on the back burner for so long.

The question to ask yourself now is: what are your questions? What are you most interested in at this point in your life? If you are still interested in your former line of work, not just because it seems the quickest way to a paycheck, then answer this: Exactly what is it that fascinates you about it? Is there something on the cutting edge of your job or industry that you naturally and authentically want to know more about? On the other hand, if you have grown weary of your old roles and playgrounds, what really lights you up now? What industries, lines of work, areas of technology, or even charitable causes naturally draw you into conversations for the simple enjoyment of learning?

When we're in a job, we rarely have the opportunity to explore the forefront of our field, much less other areas of "outside" interest, because we just have so much to do. This is your opportunity! Your passions and fascinations are your pan to sift for gold!

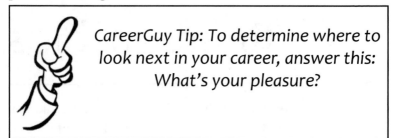

CareerGuy Tip: To determine where to look next in your career, answer this: What's your pleasure?

What if you found that you could leverage the same skills, talents, and aptitudes utilized in a field you've grown tired of in a completely new line of work that fits your updated passions and interests? Too often, folks live segmented, dual-reality lives in which their skills, talents, and aptitudes get used in their work life, but don't bridge over to what they really care about.

Let me share a story. A client had just moved to Los Angeles from the East Coast where she was the chief information technology officer (that is, head computer geek) for a $50-million manufacturing company. Like so many other myopic clients who first believe they are stuck in what they've done before, she thought her only option was to find another IT role in a manufacturing operation. However, an interesting prospect arose during our coaching process.

I utilize a particular "classifieds exercise" with my clients to help them discover their deepest passions and interest. It's a simple exercise in which they pull out all the words and phrases in the want ads that interest them. They are not looking for positions they would apply for, but rather, simply reading all the ads from every field to see what words move or inspire them.

For example, someone might circle "Work at the Beach!" because, outside of their specific industry or field, they have a strong interest in the water or coastline environments. This process is similar to a Rorschach (ink blot) test used by psychologists to assess a client's innermost perceptions of the world. Rather than assessing an ink blot, however, people mine the want ads for words and phrases that point to deep interests they may have deleted from their consciousness because of a mistaken perception that they couldn't make a living at it.

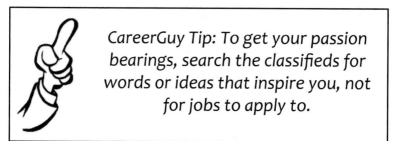

CareerGuy Tip: To get your passion bearings, search the classifieds for words or ideas that inspire you, not for jobs to apply to.

This particular client circled "Help underprivileged kids ride horseback." She said she had always had an interest in the welfare of kids and non-profit charitable causes, but had never had the time to look into it. We used this insight, along with others, to help her redirect her career into areas of fuller personal enthusiasm.

Though the exercise was not necessarily geared towards her getting a job from the ads, she did decide to simply volunteer for this particular organization because of her reawakened passion to work with kids. Interestingly enough, when she met with the director to simply ask questions about the organization and set herself up to volunteer, the conversation uncovered the fact that they were planning a nationwide expansion and specifically needed someone to set up their internal IT infrastructure!

I relate this story to demonstrate that a multitude of ways exist in which we can align our work with our passions. It *is* possible to merge our bread-and-butter world with what lights us up. In so doing, we create our own personal heaven on earth. We just need to learn ways of *creating relationships based on questions rather than our need for a job.*

To elaborate further, consider this diagram:

First, there are those functions that you do best, that you're really good at. Then, there are those activities that you love the most, where your passions lie. And, to support either or both of those, there's the necessity of compensation from the market. The ideal—and what I believe we're here to resolve and magnify—is to arrive at our own personal "Sweet Spot."

In your Sweet Spot, you are doing what you are really good at in an area of strong, passionate interest and the market is paying you handsomely for it. In your Sweet Spot, you've given up the world of duality which says that your passions and interests are luxury items that you reserve for nights and weekends (which you never actually get to). In your Sweet Spot, you've accepted that there are ways to bring your passions into alignment with your skills in new and interesting ways…and you've found them!

 CareerGuy Tip: Your real "job" in life is to find your Sweet Spot, to cultivate it, to live in it, and to express from it.

Rather than consider this only theoretically, let's do a bit of examination, to get you thinking about *your life!* Grab your Career Transformation Insights Journal again, and let's answer a few more questions.

Finding Your Sweet Spot

For this fun and enlightening exercise, I suggest you engage in it graphically, rather than simply using a linear question-and-answer format. So, turn your notebook sideways and first just draw those previous circles connecting the way they do, and leave plenty of room on the page outlying the circles so that you can write out your answers to the items listed.

There's something about seeing it all together that can help form the mental bridges that we want to start building. And don't be shy about doing this exercise on a much bigger sheet, or poster board, if you want. That might even be a good idea, so as to have something to put on the wall in your office or bedroom to keep you thinking on this exploration.

First, let's look at the left circle, What You Do Best. Though some of the items may appear to be duplicates, different words can have different meanings and trigger different thoughts for each of us. So, following some basic definitions from Merriam-Webster.com, take a few moments to jot down in the same order beside your left circle your:

Talents: the natural endowments of a person; a special athletic, creative, or artistic aptitude; general intelligence or mental power, ability.

Skills: a learned power of doing something competently; a developed aptitude or ability.

Competencies: the quality or state of being competent; proper or rightly pertinent; having requisite or adequate ability or qualities; fit.

Aptitudes: inclination, tendency; a natural ability; talent; capacity for learning; general suitability.

Abilities: the quality or state of being able; competence in doing; skill; natural aptitude or acquired proficiency.

Gifts: a notable capacity, talent, or endowment.

Expertise: the skill of an expert: having, involving, or displaying special skill or knowledge derived from training or experience.

Proficiencies: advancement in knowledge or skill; the quality or state of being proficient; well advanced in an art, occupation, or branch of knowledge.

Knacks: a clever way of doing something; a special ready capacity that is hard to analyze or teach.

Next, let's look at the left circle, What You Love. This can be a slightly more difficult inventory to take because we are often so focused on what we *have to do* than what it is we really *want to do* (or simply get pleasure out of doing for the sake of it).

In my work with people, I often find that people are so far removed from their passions that they can't even think of what those might be. This is a sad statement on our task-focused, doing-driven world that we aren't even in touch with our inner being and what lights us up.

What You Love is generally the things that we have on our "luxury list"…the items we will get to when there's enough time (right!). We often relegate these activities or interests to nights or weekends, and then get so busy with other stuff that we don't get to them. They may be "someday" items, or simply things that we have felt forced to put aside so as to "grow up" and take care of our responsibilities. Remembering, resurrecting, or reviving our passions might be a bit confronting, but better late than never, yes?

Even if you feel like rushing past this section, I invite you to give yourself the gift of pushing beyond any discomfort and allowing yourself to inquire into and list out your:

Passions: a strong liking or desire for or devotion to some activity, object, or concept; the state or capacity of being acted on by external agents or forces. [I personally love this part!]

Enthusiasms: strong excitement of feeling; ardor; something inspiring zeal or fervor.

Delights: a high degree of gratification; joy; something that gives great pleasure.

Hobbies: a pursuit outside one's regular occupation engaged in especially for relaxation.

Interests: a feeling that accompanies or causes special attention to an object or class of objects; concern; something that arouses such attention.

Dreams: a strongly desired goal or purpose; something that fully satisfies a wish; ideal.

Pastimes: something that amuses and serves to make time pass agreeably; diversion.

Obsessions: a persistent disturbing preoccupation with an often unreasonable idea or feeling; compelling motivation.

Pursuits: an activity that one engages in as a vocation, profession, or avocation; occupation.

Now that you have graphically listed out, to the best of your ability (don't worry, you'll think of more later), the elements comprising the top two circles, you want to start allowing the idea to creep into your consciousness that it's actually possible—yes, even for you!—that these two worlds can meet up in ways that you've never thought of.

Who knows exactly how they'll merge—we're not worried about that. That information will come as you learn more about how to tap into the knowledge and insights of the world around you in an effective way. The first step is simply to open yourself up to the idea that there are ways you know not of (yet) where these often seemingly disparate aspects of yourself can come together in amazing ways.

As you move forward through the book, and the whole point of this chapter in particular, you will see that your real job isn't to "figure it out" as we all think we can do. No, your job is to come up with questions...questions that you'll ask people far and wide, folks who know something about these areas, and, often and surprisingly, folks who may not know a single thing about these areas! But it's in the questions that you will be able to tap into a grander mind than your own to get the answers that will make all the difference.

 *CareerGuy Tip: You don't have to "figure out" your next career move. Just become question-able about what interests you.*

And, of course, we need to add in the final bottom circle because, in the end, we do need to pay the electric bill while we're shining our light! So, for now, just begin to allow yourself to consider the various ways in which you could bring your merged top circles to the market. Perhaps another corporate role is the way. Have you too long put aside an inner urge to take your merged upper circles in a more entrepreneurial route? Until you're clear on the area of upper-circle overlap, it's harder to know the route to go, but it's at least worth taking a moment to write out the ideas you've had in each area, or to create some if you haven't.

Corporate Employment: What do you enjoy most about working for others? What does this avenue of bringing your meshed upper circles to market afford you? What are the pros and the cons for you of this structure of worklife?

Self-Employment: Have you ever been self-employed? What are the pros and cons of that structure of worklife for you? If not, have you ever had that inkling for yourself? Has fear or uncertainty stopped you from taking the risk? What might make it worth it for you?

Building a Company: Beyond mere self-employment, have you ever considered building something bigger from the ground up, or maybe buying into an existing business? Do you know the world of capital or would you want to learn it? Are you interested in what it takes to not only build something from inception, but also be the person with whom the buck stops? What are the pros and cons of this structure of possible worklife for you?

Don't get dismayed. This doesn't all get worked out overnight. This is only to get you thinking outside of any boxes in which you've held your roles, jobs, professions, or working structures in the past. The answers will come when you've been out effectively asking the questions. Right now, simply realize that there's more power in being a "questionable" person than in trying to figure it out yourself.

My friend Richard Bolles, best-selling author of *What Color Is Your Parachute?*, tells a story of a man who had sorted out that the three areas he was most interested in and skilled at in life were psychiatry, plants, and carpentry. So, he went out to talk to people about those areas to hopefully find a way in which they could merge. One of the many people he spoke with was a psychiatrist. In asking him how these areas could possibly merge, the psychiatrist replied that there is an area of psychiatry dealing with catatonic patients wherein the patients would respond to plants but not to humans. They felt some kind of caring for the plants, as if the plant needed them. So, he suggested that the man go explore that area of psychiatry. The man then asked him, "But what about the carpentry?" to which the psychiatrist responded, "Just build the planter boxes!"

On the way to finding our personal Sweet Spot, sometimes we have to accept that, for the moment, we may live in only two merged circles. This can occur when we're doing something we do best simply for the money (not the love), or when we're doing something we do best and love, but the lights are being shut off due to not earning.

The juggling of finding our Sweet Spot—where all three merge, our uniquely personal segment of heavenly career—is an ongoing process, and simply a part of a life well-lived. There are no magic tricks that instantaneously land you in your Sweet Spot, but *it is possible to get there*…and the journey is half the fun!

I encourage folks to get into a multi-job mindset until they find themselves in their Sweet Spot. Have you ever had two or three jobs at the same time? Many of us, whether as students or even as adults, have experienced what it's like to juggle more than one career situation. As a matter of fact, in the last 15 to 20 years, the term "portfolio career" has been used to describe folks who juggle more than one job at a time…often due to simply having so many varied interests that there's not a full commitment to only one.

If you consider that, until you land into your Sweet Spot, your second, part-time job is to *pursue* your Sweet Spot, then one day you will eventually find yourself there. This means that when you get home from working the job that pays you based on your skills, not your interests, you spend at least an hour in the evenings or a few hours on the weekend figuring out ways to move into your Sweet Spot.

And, as many of us know from having second jobs, you can't just get home from your main job and say, "I'm too tired, I'm not going in tonight." You have to show up, rain or shine. This is the same discipline that we all must employ to negotiate our way into Sweet Spot careers.

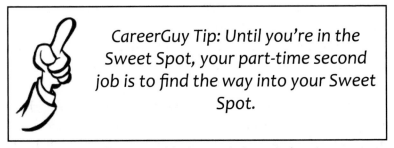

CareerGuy Tip: Until you're in the Sweet Spot, your part-time second job is to find the way into your Sweet Spot.

Our Sweet Spot would obviously be our A-job: our main point of career focus. But, whether we have to do a B-job, C-job, or D-job until we can merge our circles into our personal Sweet Spot, the challenge, as Winston Churchill said in a speech at the Harrow School in England, is that we must "never give in—never, never, never, never!" We must continue our search until we are seated in our Sweet Spot of purposeful fulfillment. It's why we came here! And guess what: It can change in time, so it's really a lifelong process: Sweet-Spot maintenance.

A Sweet-Spot maintenance program would include always being aware of where we are in the diagram and, even if we are in our Sweet Spot for the moment, staying abreast of our next level of unfolding interests or passions.

Perhaps it's an obsolete idea we grew up with that we are supposed to find that "one thing" that we do for the rest of our lives, call it our "career," and never waver from it. That might be the case, when there is so much continual expansion within an area that it never fails to merge our greater skills and passions will all our financial needs. However, more often than not, human beings are growing and evolving, shedding off old skins of past interests and values and ever-expanding into newer, fresher, more fascinating objects of career affection. Therefore, it is important, for an ever-increasing experience of fulfillment, to be willing and able to notice if our Sweet Spot has gone stale and to put the intention and attention into reframing it.

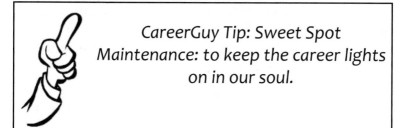

CareerGuy Tip: Sweet Spot Maintenance: to keep the career lights on in our soul.

But Sweet-Spot maintenance is down the road, once you've learned to manage your efforts and relationships to at least get into your Sweet Spot in the first place. Your task for now is to come up with the top three to five areas of current passionate interest for you—whether related to your past work and activities or not—and to create research projects based on those interests.

Here are a few deeper exercises to help you get in touch with your current passions and interests. Pull out your Career Transformation Insights Journal again, and journal a bit on these thoughts...

1. **What if Money or Career Didn't Matter? (Freebird Exercise.)** I know, I know...from the outset, this question is preposterous, right? How could money or career not matter? Well, you and I know they do and we need to pay that electric bill. But what price is having the lights on *at home* if they're out *where we really live*, in the soul of our being?

   Remember that Thoreau quote about most people living lives of quiet desperation? Maybe that's because the light is out where they really live. So, this is a worthwhile question to ask if you're up for something bigger than quiet desperation. It's also a nice divining rod to use as a guide in the development of research projects.

   What three things would you be spending your time engaging in or talking to people about? Get yourself in the mindset, and write out a few things that would warrant your time and attention.

2. **Passionate Interests "Ink Blot" (Classifieds Exercise.)** This is the exercise I mentioned earlier, whereby my client had an opportunity to bring her skills (IT infrastructure) into an area of dormant and neglected passion (the welfare of kids and teens). In many ways, this is similar to a Rorschach ink blot exercise, often used by mental health professionals to analyze a person's personality characteristics and emotional functioning. Similar because it gets underneath the conscious awareness to highlight underlying elements of importance.

Basically, as previously mentioned, we aren't always as in touch with our true, dormant, or latent passions as we are our to-do list because we're so darn busy doing what we think we *have to do!* Therefore, we need to approach this discovery in more of a stealth way: sneaking up on it behind our conscious mind, which would tell us to quit wasting time.

Here's the exercise: Back in the days of newspapers and classifieds sections, I would have clients start at A and go all the way through to Z, reading all the job opportunities, looking simply for **words and phrases** that interested them and circling those words or phrases. Be clear, this is *not about looking for a job you would either be qualified for or apply for:* simply identifying words and phrases that interest you in any way, and circling them.

In today's online world, the best way to accomplish this, while allowing for the same feel of being able to see *all* the ads rather than just the ones in a particular field, is to go on Craigslist and look under the "Jobs" section. Use it just like you would a newspaper, starting at A and working your way down. Begin with the "Accounting + Finance" section and look through the ads for the last couple of days, while jotting down down in your Career Transformation Insights Journal or copy and paste into a Microsoft Word document the words and phrases that interest you. Then move to the next section, and the next, going all the way through to the "Writing/Editing" section.

Yes, this will take a good hour or so, but the introspection that comes out of it is completely worth it.

Here's an example:

While disregarding the type of job or field of each ad, as you read through the ads from beginning to end, let's say you see the phrase "strong team player." The idea of teamwork has always interested you, and you have thrived in those environments. So you jot down that phrase in your journal…or, better yet, and in order to prepare for the second half of the exercise, you copy and paste that phrase into a Word document.

Then you see an ad that says "Heavy travel, including international" which also piques your interest, given you've always loved travel and seeing foreign countries. You copy it as well.

You continue on, from A to Z, reading through all the ads and writing down only the words and phrases that grab your attention. It may be a preference for something that you're consciously aware of, or it may bring up old, forgotten interests or fantasy ideas that you've written off for whatever reason.

In the end, you'll end up with a list of words and phrases such as this:

strong team player	we have a lot of fun
heavy travel, including international	business development manager
physical	generate new revenue
personal and financial wellness	build client relationships
balance	requires traveling
working smarter, not harder	implement
more time for the truly important things	communicate
We don't wait for life to happen to us, we make life happen around us.	organize
marketing/advertising	watch
Los Angeles	social
business management	professional manner
directors of learning centers	highly motivated
candidates seeking equity in a business of their own	referrals
leadership skills	statistical tracking
marketing experience	San Diego
we give progressive benefits	outgoing

The next step—and you don't want to think of this while gathering data—is to organize all of these words and phrases into the categories they seem to be pointing to. No two persons' categories are exactly the same, yet some similar categories begin to show up rather regularly. Look to see what categories are naturally implied by the words and phrases you pulled.

Here's a possible categorization of the previous list:

Qualities to Exhibit	Duties/ Responsibilities	Skills Utilized/ Required
strong team player	heavy travel, including international	marketing/ advertising
we have a lot of fun	physical	business management
social	marketing/advertising	leadership skills
professional manner	business management	marketing experience
highly motivated	business development manager	business development manager
outgoing	generate new revenue	generate new revenue
	build client relationships	build client relationships
	requires traveling	implement
	implement	communicate
	communicate	organize
	organize	watch
	watch	social
	statistical tracking	statistical tracking

Workplace Environment	Company Mindset	Values
balance	working smarter, not harder attitudes	more time for the truly important things in life
we have a lot of fun	We don't wait for life to happen to us, we make life happen around us.	we have a lot of fun
requires traveling		build client relationships
social	we have a lot of fun	social
professional manner	build client relationships	professional manner
Roles	**Perks/Draws/Offerings**	**Industry**
directors of learning centers	heavy travel, including international	personal and financial wellness
business development manager	candidates seeking equity in a business of their own	marketing/advertising
	we give progressive benefits	business management
	we have a lot of fun	
	requires traveling	
	social	
Company Objectives	**Geographic Location**	
we have a lot of fun	Los Angeles	
build client relationships	San Diego	
referrals		

This exercise isn't based on an exact science, mind you. It's more creative, drawing on the right side of the brain. Consider it more like a painting, in which you throw together some of your favorite shapes and colors to see what image arises.

The particular categories/subject headings you come up with and the way you sort the words/ phrases is rather subjective, often depending on the context in which the words/phrases occur, the meanings you place upon the words, and your desires. Notice how travel shows up as a perk/draw/ offering here whereas, for some, it would only be an element of duties/responsibilities.

Sometimes there are repetitive items that you've extracted, which is good: it shows how much that element means to you (for example, travel). Also, at times, an item may fall into more than one category, such as social, which, in this case, can be categorized as a quality to exhibit, a particular skill utilized/required, a characteristic of a desired workplace environment, and even a value.

There are three main reasons for conducting this exercise at least once, and a few times during a couple of weeks is even better.

☞ The exercise gets you outside of a first thoughts/ immediacy kind of thinking and tweaks your career mind with ideas and possibilities you wouldn't usually consider.

☞ It can be used as a roadmap and divining rod to start your investigation of paths heretofore untraveled and unconsidered. This is particularly helpful when designing your research projects for a systematic stealth campaign.

☞ Such an exercise begins to reveal patterns in your core interests and can serve as a litmus test for the viability of other opportunities that may be presented to you through traditional means: openings you hear about, ads you come across, and so on. Basically, it helps you get clear about what you'd be involved in if you had your druthers… and that is a place of powerful career choice that you always want to strive for.

3. **Your Current Career or Occupation (Resparking Exercise):** Back in Principle #2, when initially describing research projects, I mentioned a client who hailed from the theme park industry. He had designed his stealth campaign based upon a question of interest to him that was on the cutting edge of his industry. It wasn't just another day-at-the-office kind of idea, but something that he was really passionate about investigating.

Don't think that, just because you might find yourself at a crossroads, maybe even for the first time allowing yourself to question what you're really fascinated by, that it means you absolutely have to turn elsewhere, beyond your current industry. If your passions aren't there, yes, do the courageous thing and consider your passion-based alternatives. However, give yourself an opportunity to also consider if there is something inside of or related to your current field that actually could interest you. If you simply gave yourself the right to step up beyond the mundane of what you're currently doing and view the work/industry/trends from a higher perspective, what might you see?

In other words, do you believe that you are worthy of having a vision? Or is a vision reserved only for certain privileged and "special people" out there... those who were born a certain way, had certain education, fell into certain opportunities, or in some other way had privileges that you didn't?

CareerGuy Tip: Ask yourself: Am I worthy of having a vision?

A vision could include anything from creating a smoother workflow process for greater productivity on a production line to entertaining a game-changing and innovative idea that turns an industry upside down. A vision could impact only those involved in a certain process or function of a specialized field, or could have multiple impacts spanning companies, industries, or even world trade.

So, before you bag your current gig altogether, given that you currently know a little bit about a little bit, explore some "How about..." and "What if we..." and "Why can't this..." questions that really pique your interest. Sometimes the "mastery" of a field requires reinventing the field for yourself, and your reason for being in it.

Just as a marriage or other relationship needs attention, creativity, and fresh perspective to make it vital and fulfilling, a career can often call for some romantic dates, growth experiences, and even renewing of vows. Sometimes you need to remind yourself of what got you there in the first place, go back to those core desires—underneath the blasé busy-ness than has had your nose too close to the ground—and see if there is a way to reinvent the passionate intrigue that got you into that steady relationship originally.

You owe it to yourself to explore profession(al) relationship counseling if that is what's truly in order.

 *CareerGuy Tip: Ask yourself: Is my current career worth saving? Is there a chance for renewed sugar and spice?*

Here are some questions to ask yourself as you consider if this romance is worth saving. Take a few minutes to explore…

1. How did I end up doing what I do right now anyway? Was it due to a conscious choice, or simply a fluke? Had I put much thought into it beforehand, or was it something that just fell in my lap?

2. Did I ever really enjoy it? Did I once enjoy it, but now it seems the honeymoon is over? Do I still really enjoy it passionately?

3. What is it that appealed to me about it initially? What kept my interest? What aspects of this work/industry/profession still truly appeal to me?

4. Are there elements at the cutting edge of my current field that fascinate me? If so, what are they?

5. What ideas have occurred to me, perhaps only in passing, for making my line of work more efficient, enjoyable, farther-reaching, trendy, impactful, or game-changing?

6. If I could be more at the forefront of new ideas and innovations affecting my current field, what would I want to participate in?

7. If I could play at these broader-vision levels, would I like to stay in this industry?

8. Are there lines of work related to what I currently do that have areas of intrigue or fascination for me, in which my current associated industry knowledge could be an asset?

9. How do I see my current knowledge impacting what I would like to do in that related area, and what do I need to and want to know more about?

10. Am I really kidding myself? Am I only considering reviving a dead vocation because I'm afraid to go out and research brand-new areas of interest? Am I simply planning to make do, doing the same old same old, because I think I'm locked in, I'm too old to make a total career shift, or I'm a proponent of the old adage, "You can't teach an old dog new tricks?" (If yes to any of these questions, [Buzzer Sound]! No pass! Go back and really work the Freebird and Classifieds exercises. You don't get to wimp out on being the most useful and alive for yourself—much less humanity—because of your fear!)

Investing some quality time in yourself by engaging in these exercises should evoke ideas, insights, and inquiries that get your heart pumping a little faster...or break up the flatline if it has stopped beating altogether.

At a minimum, you should be able to arrive at three to five possibilities for interested inquiry. Once you've isolated those areas of passionate interest, write out 20 questions you want answers to in each subject. That shouldn't be hard at all because you're authentically interested in this stuff, remember?!

NOW, TO BECOME QUESTION-ABLE

A few potential areas for interest exploration and possible questions based on the previous Classifieds Exercise might be:

Wellness Industry	Business Development	Travel
What is hottest these days in the wellness industry? In what ways do personal and financial wellness coincide?	What do organizations look for when attracting strong business development managers?	How does one travel widely and yet live a balanced life?
How is traditional marketing, advertising and business development contoured to fit a wellness-oriented community such as this?	Where might my background and experience be an asset to an organization looking to develop strong client relationships?	How does a talent for relationship development, revenue generation, and an interest in heavy travel come together?
What are the organizations and/or movements that are at the forefront of this industry, and how are they reaching out to gain awareness?	What are the leading organizations that operate from a balanced and professional yet social and fun environment?	What are the worldwide organizations that focus on business management or marketing and advertising?
In what ways or roles is travel and learning a part of this industry?	Who are the organizations best-known for fostering teamwork among a driven and highly outgoing staff?	What international organizations based outside of North America may have business development needs throughout this region?
What opportunities exist to infuse the elements of fun and play into the workplace?	In what ways in the market can one work smart instead of hard and gain a piece of the action/equity?	What worldwide causes are developing learning centers?
(Another 15 questions)	(Another 15 questions)	(Another 15 questions)

Again, notice that this isn't an exact science. Yet, the inner ideas and fascinations illuminated by the Classifieds Exercise gives you a jumping-off point for lots of inquiries into these areas.

The previous possible lines of questioning are just a few to be mined from the full palette of career colors that arose through the exercise. Notice that one line of inquiry is based on an industry segment (wellness industry), another explores a role to fulfill (business development), and another is focused on an element of duties and responsibilities to fulfill (travel). There's easily another 15 questions to ask in each area, and many more areas that could be mined out of the results of the overall Classifieds Exercise. Add this plethora of inquiries to those developed from the Freebird and Resparking Exercises, and you have a huge reason to be out talking to people! You become a very "question-able" person!

NOTE: For even more help with identifying your particular Sweet Spot, see a special eBook that delves into greater detail, *Finding the S Spot*, at *www.CareerGuy.com*.

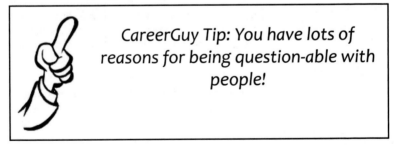

CareerGuy Tip: You have lots of reasons for being question-able with people!

Now, your job is simply to get ready to go out and talk to people in those areas of interest.

Remember, first and foremost, that you are seeking answers only because you're fascinated by the subject: not because you need a job. And, believe me, if you approach your meetings completely for this reason, you'll meet more people and actually create inroads into otherwise foreign territory simply by your passionate interest.

Principle #4: You Can Never Have too Much Information, and the Higher the Altitude, the Better

How many folks do you know who went to law school but never practiced law? How about people who invested years in an MBA, PhD, or even ministerial school who then went in a completely different direction? There's nothing wrong with that from an overall growth perspective: We all expand from every experience, and learning even for the sake of learning alone is admirable and worthwhile.

But, if you're interested in zeroing in on your Sweet Spot in the most time-efficient way, and would like to actually see income arise from that Sweet Spot, then you can never have too much information…and the time to get it is *before* you commit energy, money, or working hours to some particular career pursuit.

Have you ever had a job, or worked for a particular company, when you wish you had found out more about it *before* you took the job? Many of us have. The problem is, when you interview overtly, it's all about looking good, answering the interviewer's questions correctly, and doing whatever it takes to have the company hire you. Sounds like desperate dating, right?

When you are so transfixed on selling yourself rather than getting information about a direction or industry you are considering, you miss out on a lot—and sometimes pick bad bedfellows. There's often no way to get the full skinny through overt search. Lack of full information is a natural downfall of the traditional, overt-search beast. You're competing for the job, you feel lucky that they picked you to interview, you don't want to make waves by being pushy for more information…and so the overt-search world turns.

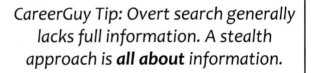

*CareerGuy Tip: Overt search generally lacks full information. A stealth approach is **all about** information.*

Compare this to a stealth approach. When you meet people based on your enthusiastic interests, completely structured around your research projects and the things you want to know, you can ask anything!

"So, what stinks about this industry?" "When are the days you would just rather pull the covers over your head?" "What trends are threatening this field?" All of those and more fit perfectly into a research project. Plus, operating this way allows you to garner much more information than you ever would through the traditional, "Please hire me!" job interview model. Again, you can never have too much information—so that's what you want to focus on obtaining.

When going out into the world of people who don't currently know you from Adam, for an effective stealth approach, you want to seek information and guidance from folks at least two levels higher than your own corporate or skill level. Someone at your own level would not be the best first contact for research, if you can avoid it. Higher "altitude" impacts attitude, aptitude, and amplitude.

 **CareerGuy Tip: Good research contacts are two levels above your own position.**

So, if you are an accounts payable manager, you'll want to approach controllers; if you are a sales manager, you'll want to approach VPs or CEOs; if you are a new graduate with a marketing degree, you'll want to approach marketing managers or chief marketing officers.

There are several reasons why you want your contacts to have altitude:

1. A higher-level person generally has a wider level of expertise, knowledge, and/or savvy.

2. A higher-level person has a wider view of trends both throughout the industry as well as within their particular organization, whereas a lower-level person will be more involved in the minutia of the moment.

3. A higher-level person will have a broader awareness of upcoming projects and directions that the department or company as a whole will be pursuing, whereas the lower-level staff will be more focused on what needs to be done *today*.

4. A higher-level person is more apt to be senior enough (in age or experience) to understand and appreciate the value of professional relationships and the role of mentoring, whereas a lower-rung worker may not be as politically astute.

5. It's a lot easier to get passed down than up if your contact wants you to meet others he thinks can further help you within his own organization.

For these reasons, you'll target the higher-level professionals in your fields of interest for your research interviews. Again, not necessarily the president or CEO; just two levels higher than the level at which you would see yourself operating.

As we discussed in the final questions development portion of Principle #3, when you have an authentic and engaging interest in something, it's never a problem to put together 20 or more questions about that subject. So, that's what you do. Write down exactly what it is you want to know about that area, field, technology, cause, and so on, to design your research projects. This will be easy, and will give you the basis for information-gathering that will provide the necessary knowledge you need, as well as the contacts to support a stealth transition.

Principle #5: A Friend in Need Doth Repulsion Breed

I hear you saying, "Okay, I can go out and ask a lot of questions, but how is that going to get me a job?" To answer that, let's revisit the gist of Principle #2, An Ounce of Research is Worth a Pound of Job Search: JUST FORGET NEEDING A JOB!

As a matter of fact, when you really get into this mindset and play this well, if someone actually begins to talk to you about an actual job opportunity within your research area, you'll respond calmly, without any nervous twitch or gleeful overexcitement at all: "Oh, an opportunity? Sure, well, I was really just seeking some answers, but sure, if you have something you'd like to discuss, I'd be happy to talk about that. Would you like to set up another time, or would you like to discuss it now?"

This isn't about being aloof. It's about being focused and knowing your own value, so you don't come across as beseeching.

In other words, if you're really focused on passionately discussing those things which truly interest you—which will be contagious, completely infecting the people you meet with—and coming from that joyful exploration rather than *need*, you're going to show up more attractively. People will naturally want to help you and, even as you assert that it's not about getting a job, they'll actually be more proactive in funneling opportunities to you!

But you can't come at it with that end in mind. You must *really* drop the "I need a job!" desperation. It may be counterintuitive for you, but years of experience have proven that it works.

CareerGuy Mantra: Approach from need, away they stampede. Approach from joy, the world will employ.

Approach from joyful inquiry and three things occur. First, when you take away the protective armor that many people wear—which shields them from the needs of others that they are afraid they can't fill—their natural tendency to help you will spontaneously emerge.

Second, when you've eliminated all indications of desperation, you'll just naturally appear as more appealing to them: like the belle of the ball who confidently, though not smugly, embodies her own value.

Third, when you speak to an area of passionate interest for you that relates to their expertise, it's like you're singing their song, and the natural enthusiasm that arises creates an emotional bond between the two of you.

Let me give you an example of how shifting your mindset away from neediness shifts your energy, which, in turn, shifts the opportunities attracted to you. A client of mine was a high-level, VP-marketing type. We completed his preliminary career inventory work, so he understood his unique value and patterns of success; we even personally "branded" him in an authentic yet catchy way, so that his verbal presentation of himself made him stand out from others, as did his branded resume.

He then proceeded to stealth forward as I instructed him—strictly to research certain topics interesting to him and to build relationships. The only problem was that he still allowed survival-mode desperation to seep into his conversations. His hints of beseeching weren't overt, but a tone of fear-based neediness limited the results he was achieving. He wasn't getting referrals based on his research (which we will discuss later), and he definitely wasn't hearing of opportunities.

As much as I coached him to "de-desperatize" himself, he continued to show up in meetings as the equivalent of an online-matchmaking-site newbie: desperate and needy for a "relationship."

One day he said, "Darrell, through all the introspective work we've done, something has become clear—I have entrepreneurism in my blood! My father was an entrepreneur. His father was an entrepreneur. My brothers and sisters are all entrepreneurs. So I've come to this conclusion: To heck with corporate jobs—I'm going to start my own business!"

He went on to purchase a couple of franchises and was happier than ever. But what matters most, and the point of the example, is that the moment he stopped "needing" a job, some interesting events occurred.

With his job search now completely behind him and out of his mind, he began receiving calls from folks he had met during his stealth campaign. He also started to receive unexpected calls on the branded resume he had placed on the Internet. Now without any attachment to landing an interview, he returned calls and discussed frankly the opportunities people presented to him, exploring the industry's and company's direction, and so on. Basically, he engaged in a lot of unattached chit-chat (a.k.a., non-desperate research).

In one instance, he told a hiring manager over the phone, "In all honesty, the role and compensation you're describing is simply far below anything I'd consider, so I don't want to waste your time by coming in." The hiring manager, probably not used to such detachment from a candidate, responded that he would be more than willing to raise the compensation significantly if he could find someone of a high caliber that warranted it...and basically pleaded for him to come in for an interview.

CareerGuy Tip: The only thing between you and the world appreciating your value is your neediness.

He actually did go in, and opened some further doors for himself, but that's beside the point. What matters is that when he "de-desperatized" himself—removing all neediness from his conversations, demeanor, and actions—the world responded immediately to this new self-perception of his value.

His internal-world *sense-of-value* shift caused an external-world *awareness-of-value* shift. He called me to say that he finally understood what I had been trying to impart for so many months. Without *need* glaring through everything he did and said, and by simply focusing on research and building authentic relationships, the world was practically begging him to come out and play.

Think about this principle in your own life, when it comes to anything you have feverishly sought (a romantic relationship, a promotion, special recognition) versus things you have coolly and calmly "attracted." It's the same lesson in all instances: What we think we need, we tend to push away because we are less our real self. We are trying too hard. But, when dropping the mask of need and standing in our own value, we can even find ourselves pursued.

> *"You need not leave your room. Remain sitting at your table and listen. You need not even listen, simply wait, just learn to become quiet, and still, and solitary. The world will freely offer itself to you to be unmasked. It has no choice; it will roll in ecstasy at your feet."*
>
> *~ Franz Kafka*

Perhaps Kafka takes it a bit far in terms of career transition—because you definitely need to be out there meeting people rather than at your table! But the spiritual energy to which he alludes is absolutely relevant: You want to meet others, while in full awareness of your own value and self-sufficiency, in a collegial rather than needy way. That is why your emphasis is to get answers to your research projects rather than hit folks up for a job.

Everyone is your friend until you see it otherwise. As a matter of fact, one of the best definitions for a friend that I've used in presentations for years comes from Webster's Dictionary: One who is not hostile! That really opens up your list of available friends to connect with, doesn't it?

Principle #6: Call Me Expert, I'll Open My Door

You may be wondering how you will actually set up these research project meetings. Easy! Just put yourself back in college when you were doing a case study, or some other time in life when you wanted to find out about something merely for the sake of learning.

First, you find people involved in that subject area, and then you make a request to meet! If you are really in the research mode/mind, this won't occur to them as weird at all...and you will come across as someone they will genuinely want to help with any information they have. It works for 22-year-old students looking for a first-time career, and it works for 50-year-old executives exploring new options.

Let's not discount the experts who may already be surrounding you in life. Besides the outer, unknown experts, a critical ingredient of an effective stealth campaign is tapping into your current network of relationships. For sure, you want to expand your network far and wide with all of the authorities and higher-ups in their respective industries. But don't discount the throngs of people *in your world right now* who have information, knowledge, contacts, and relationships *that you have no concept of* simply because you have not tapped into them effectively.

CareerGuy Tip: Right now, at your very fingertips, are contacts, knowledge, and relationships that could move your career forward.

In a thorough stealth campaign, you always want to harvest from your own fields first…because the fruit of the harvest is so much closer and just waiting to be scooped up. Even if you think you have already scoured your current relationships for all the helpful input, advice, and connections they can offer, I promise you that you haven't—because you haven't used an effective method.

What most people consider "networking" is merely telling family, friends, and neighbors, "I'm looking for a new job, so if you hear of anything, let me know!" Granted, that method is better than locking yourself in a closet, but only slightly. It makes you look like someone willing to hear about or take "anything." Plus, it fails to powerfully tap into the real knowledge and connections you have right at your fingertips through these people.

Human beings tend to get comfortable in their relationships with each other—friends, family, and neighbors—and assume to know each other well. They fail to keep deeply exploring each other's lives, activities, and changes. How you initially met someone has shaped the content of your knowing them…and you have considered that you *really* know them when now, today, you *really* don't. Yet, were you to creatively design a research project for which they would be an only-person-on-the-planet-who-could-answer-your-questions target, then you'd have a basis for connecting with them in a completely different way.

The point is this: The method you're learning right now about reaching out to meet new people based on research projects, setting up those meetings, and what you'll learn about how to conduct those meetings *is the same method to be applied to the people you already know!*

You may say, "But that's weird! I already know them. How do I conduct research with someone I already know?!" I'll show you how when I describe the "Approach Letters" you'll use to make contact with both unknown targets and friends. For now, just realize that your current close connections have information, knowledge, contacts, and relationships right now *that you are unaware of,* and only when you learn to harvest from your own fields effectively will you hit those pockets of new possibility. Plus, working the "system" on these old-time contacts gives you your sea legs for working it on those you don't know at all.

 *CareerGuy Tip: A stealth approach to your current contacts gives you practice for approaching those you don't know…and gets you goodies!*

Let's come up with a list of contacts from which to begin building your stealth campaign. Best-selling author Harvey Mackay wrote a book entitled *Dig Your Well Before You're Thirsty*, which is all about building and nurturing relationships. I want you to consider that you have put an entire *lifetime* into making connections...and your job now is to simply remember them and put them to good use!

Pull out your Career Transformation Insights Journal and let's do an inventory of the people you know...both the warm and fuzzy close contacts and the more distant, barely remembered ones. Then we'll look into the many and varied folks that you can *get to know* based on your research projects.

FINDING YOUR WELLS

Studies have shown that the average person knows approximately 600 people. That's just average. Many people know many more than that...into the thousands.

Here are a few exercises to help you become aware of the vast amount of individuals you already know, as well as the limitless folks whom you *can get to know* by using these stealth methods.

Locating Your Networks

First, realize that you are part of a multitude of networks, some that come to mind quickly and some that you don't usually think of as networks. Merriam-Webster.com defines a *network* as "a usually informally interconnected group or association of persons." For us, we're going to define a *network* as any group or environment in which you may readily recognize another or be recognized by another. In your journal, write out the categories of the networks you belong to down the page...leaving about two inches after each one.

Some of the first networks you might come up with are:

☞ Friends

☞ Family

☞ Neighbors

☞ Former coworkers/supervisors

☞ Former customers/vendors

☞ Corporate executives

☞ Alumni associations

☞ Educational settings (professors, deans, children's schools)

☞ Professional/trade associations

☞ Professionals services providers (lawyers, bankers, doctors, CPAs, therapists)

☞ Business owners (dry cleaner, gardener, hair stylist, store owner, club)

☞ Religious organizations

☞ Personal development/support groups

☞ Community groups/volunteer associations

☞ Sports activities/teams

☞ Internet social networks

But there can be many more as you really think about where you would recognize others and where you would be recognized...

Places You Frequent

☞ **The gym:** Perhaps you've never actually said hello to that person who is always working out beside you, but she would surely recognize you.

☞ **Neighborhood coffee shop:** Again, maybe you haven't actually met them, but there are lots of people you see all the time.

Inherited Networks

☞ **Your spouse's or partner's networks in all of the previous examples:** By association, you have an inroad with these folks simply because of the name recognition of your spouse, whereby you are easily "recognized."

☞ **Your parents' networks in all of the previous examples:** We're always going to be someone's kid, no matter how old we get…and this is also an avenue of easily inherited recognition.

☞ **Kids' schools and activities:** The kids with whom your child interacts also have parents and guardians, and these are easy connections to make because you are "recognized" by that association.

Mining Your Networks

Now that you have a good sense of the many networks you belong to, you want to start digging and listing all the names (or faces if you don't know the names) of the individuals who would comprise each group.

It's important that you look *all the way back* in each category when you do this exercise. In other words, your friends and your customers or vendors from jobs from years past won't immediately come to mind, but you want to mine them. I usually give my workshop participants a little game to see who can come up with the most people in each category within three minutes. The winner receives a standing ovation. Get a timer or look at the second counter on your watch and set it for three minutes. Fill out as many names/faces in the two inches you have under each category.

Of course, you can take more than three minutes, but it's a good start as a game. When participants come up with anywhere from 30 to 60 names within those three minutes, my encouragement is for them to then go home and give it a good 30 minutes—because they'll likely come up with 10 times as many! Whether you take three or 30 minutes right now, the point is to get them all out so that you can begin to think of creative ways to tap into these networks for research.

Contacts Wish List

If you took the time to analyze your Sweet Spot in Principle #3, as well as engage in the Freebird, Classifieds, and Resparking Exercises, you undoubtedly came up with some areas of passionate interest that you would like to explore.

They could be within your current field, perhaps involving some cutting-edge aspects of the industry you hadn't allowed yourself to reach for. It might involve a role or position that you want to investigate. Or, perhaps you got clear that where you're at is considering an area or function totally unrelated to what you've done in the past.

Either way, now you want to create a Contacts Wish List of the folks you'd like to engage in conversation around these items of interest. You also want to take into account the coaching of Principle #4: to reach for the higher-altitude connections. If you're going to create relationships out of thin air, you might as well have them be with folks who have the attitude, aptitude, and amplitude to best help you.

In your Career Transformation Insights Journal, write out each area/item of potential exploration along the top line of a sheet of paper, allowing three items per sheet. So, if you have six items, you want to write them out across two sheets.

Then, start doing some basic research (online and by talking to your friends), to find out which top organizations are involved in each of those areas, as well as the best resources to tap into. Begin by listing at least 10 organizations and resources that stand out in that field or item of inquiry.

For example, using the few potential areas for research that came out of the Classifieds Exercise demonstrated in Principle #3, I took just a few minutes to simply search the first few Internet page results for these phrases. I found industry summaries and a plethora of links that allowed me, in virtually no time at all, to quickly compile this list of 10 organizations or resources to possibly research, either for contacts or further information leading to contacts. (This is not an endorsement of these organizations or resources, only a possible list of organizations to mine for contacts. There are thousands more that one could find and mine in each area of this particular example.)

Your sheet might look like this:

Wellness Industry	Business Development	Travel
Various corporate wellness consultants (paid ads)	Generic business development position descriptions	PasadenaCal.org Major and minor travel agencies in my area
MarketResearchReports.com (Wellness industry reports)	A Guide to Business Development 2.0 by ReadWriteWeb.com	U.S. Travel Association TravelIndustryWire.com
bx.businessweek.com/wellness-industry/ (A listing of various articles worldwide)	Learn.linkedin.com/business-development/ (showing how to make connections through LinkedIn)	Travel + Leisure Magazine Tourism-Review.com
A full 34-page .PDF report on the Fitness & Wellness industry by the Merriman Curhan Ford investment group	MBDA.gov (Minority Business Development Agency) Various state business development centers	ICTA (Institute of Certified Travel Agents) CLIA (Cruise Lines International Association) WTMLondon.com
A 2002 book, The Wellness Revolution, by Paul Zane Pilzer	BusinessWithoutBorders.com	International Airline Travel Association
Dozens of multi-level marketing organizations	BDIOnline.com (Business Development Institute)	
HealthandWellness Association.com	WDBC.org (Women's Business Development Center)	
CorporateWellness Magazine.com	Beansprout.co (Channel Partners Matchmaking)	
Pulsecor.com medical device technology	whartonsbdc.wharton.upenn.edu/ (Wharton Small Business Development Center)	
The Bali Spa & Wellness Association		

The breadth of your search results can be narrowed, if necessary, by putting in your city or area after the specific search term. Of course, some top search results could be simply due to savvy search engine optimization, so it pays to dig beyond the first few pages.

This isn't rocket science, as many folks perform Internet searches every day. However, as you'll see, I have pulled out various organizations and resources in which to dig to find contacts to connect with.

☞ If it's a local business, such as a particular health club or travel agency, I could research or call to find the name of the manager or owner.

☞ If it's a corporation, I can research the company Website or call to find out the name of a high-level executive in charge of my area of expertise.

☞ If it's a trade or professional association, I can find out the name of the person who directs the local chapter.

☞ If it's a major Website or governmental organization located elsewhere, I can call for guidance on who would be a designated person to reach in my area.

The point is…the world is your oyster once you know what you want to become question-able about. All you have to do is dig up the folks you will question. Then, you simply put together an Approach Letter outlining your request to meet with them based on your questions.

 *CareerGuy Tip: The world is your oyster, when you know what to be question-able about.*

In Principle #1, I asked if you believe people really want to help others. I hope you agreed with me that they do. If you didn't, this method will be very challenging for you...but you can shift that mindset. I offer some affirmations at the end of the book that can help.

If you agree people want to be helpful, great. But remember, as I said before, they will only engage their helping nature in situations in which they believe they can win. They will avoid situations in which they think they could lose.

An additional barrier to people being helpful to others is time: nobody has enough, and if you need a lot from them, you're out of luck. Therefore, in approaching others to assist in your research projects, you must dismantle these two barriers from the outset— their desire to win and not lose, and their time constraints.

To demonstrate by example, let's take a situation in which you are an engineer and have decided to explore the renewable energy field. It fascinates you and is a cause/movement/industry that you're passionate about promoting. Perhaps you currently know very little about it; only enough to jump on the Internet and perform a simple subject search.

Let's say you find solar, wind, and alternative fuels development companies in your area and you want to gather information about those sectors of the industry. Which of the two "Approach Letters" will net you the best chance of meeting the chief engineer, Thomas?

Approach Letter #1

Thomas O'Malley, Chief Engineer
EcoFan, Inc.
11467 Hillcrest Drive
High Pointe, OR 97031

Dear Thomas,

Having spent the last 18 years in the field of engineering, I am a seasoned professional with experience in both design and operations.

I am interested in EcoFan's positive impact on the environment and believe my skills and capabilities would be of value to the company and its direction.

I would like to schedule a time at your convenience to meet and discuss my background and how it may serve the continued progress of EcoFan. I have enclosed my resume and will call your office in the next week to set up a time that will work for you.

Sincerely,
Joe JobSeeker

Approach Letter #2

Thomas O'Malley, Chief Engineer
EcoFan, Inc.
11467 Hillcrest Drive
High Pointe, OR 97031

Dear Thomas,

I am writing to you because of your unique position within the renewable energy industry. I have observed the development of EcoFan as a significant player within the wind energy field, and am particularly fascinated by the new technologies being adapted to wind turbines in the Central Valley.

Frankly, I don't know as much as I'd like about the direction wind energy is headed in the Pacific Northwest, which is why I'm seeking information. I'm specifically researching the engineering requirements for municipalities to take advantage of these growing technologies.

Because of your role as a leader within this burgeoning field, I thought you might be able to give me some information regarding my research. Please be aware, I don't expect you to have a job or to know of any. However, five to 10 minutes of your time would be most helpful as I gather information on the subject.

Hoping you could offer me five to 10 minutes of your time when most convenient for you, I'll call your office in the next week to schedule an appointment. I have enclosed my pertinent information, just so you know a bit about me.

Sincerely,
Rita Researcher

Which approach do you believe stands the best chance of a meeting with Tom? Obviously, Approach #2. Let's discuss the reasons why.

1. Approach #1—what the vast majority of folks send out in job search mode—has "I NEED A JOB!" written overtly all over it. On the off chance that Tom might actually have a need in his department, it *might* get shuffled off to HR with a note that says, "Please screen for possible interview." Yet, that's on the off chance…and then you're left with a first contact of the HR department. More often, unless a company is either growing exponentially or is an absolute hellhole where people are leaving in droves, there isn't going to be a position currently open. In that case, under Approach #1, your resume still gets shuffled off to HR, with no note whatsoever, or may end up in a file somewhere (digital, flat, or round) to be totally forgotten.

2. Approach #1 is all about "I"—me, myself, and "I"—and each sentence begins with that most-important, personal pronoun. Joe is clearly attempting to be interesting, rather than interested. Oh sure, Joe is interested in a job…but it's all about what he wants and needs, and he's trying hard to sell himself because of that need. His letter offers the premise, "Do you have a job for me?" If the answer is "Possibly," then there might be a meeting down the road, long after the gauntlet of HR processing, initial screening, and so on. If the answer (more likely) is "No, not right now,"

then, again, this overture is quickly forgotten in some file.

3. Approach #2 presents a valid interest in a subject/topic of common interest: the tapping of wind energy in the area. Having a research project forces Rita to be interested rather than interesting… and the more detailed and granular she can present her research project, the more it has legs to warrant a legitimate information-gathering campaign that Tom might be willing to participate in. In other words, a broad general interest in green energy is less likely to capture the enthusiastic attention of Tom than a specific, in-depth interest in "the new technologies being adapted to wind turbines in the Central Valley." The more specific your research, the more credible it is perceived as simply research.

4. Rita's language in Approach #2 sets up Tom as an expert in his field, and his company as the leader in the industry. She attempts to have him feel that he's the only person on the planet who could give her the information she needs. She appeals to something we all have: ego. This is not to say that shameless sucking up will get Tom to "hold all calls" just for Rita, but notice that the little flavor of expert ego-stroking creates a more attractive approach to requesting a meeting.

5. In Approach #2, Rita actually disclaims that she expects Tom to have a job for her, or to know of one, which addresses that little voice speaking in the back of his head wondering

just that. He definitely doesn't want to be put in an uncomfortable position to be hit up for a job he may not have, so this takes the pressure off…allowing him to simply consider whether he has the time to be helpful in her quest for information. He may or may not have the time, but there's a much stronger chance he'll offer it if he can squeeze it in knowing that he is just being contacted for information. Notice the subtlety that Rita employs by not referring to her enclosure as a "resume" as Joe did, but rather, her "pertinent information." Tom would naturally want to know a bit about the person contacting him, but the word "resume" takes the mind in a different direction.

6. In Approach #2, Rita asks for only five to 10 minutes, whereas Joe is setting Tom up for what could be a lengthy and cumbersome interview process if he accepts. Frankly, Tom doesn't have any extra time, but if followed up with, poked, prodded, and engaged by phone a bit, he might cough up five to 10 minutes for Rita. Truth be told, if Rita follows the meeting format I'm going to share with you in Principle #8, "The 5 Stages of a Stealth Interview," she'll be there for more than an hour…and he'll be tickled that she came by!

Clearly, Rita rules the roost when it comes to the chance of meeting Tom at EcoFan. But does that mean, because she wrote a better letter, that Tom will immediately jump on the phone and call her in? No! Again, he's a very busy guy. But if Rita begins a consistent and steady follow-up process after this letter—and all the other letters sent out to even more "only-person-on-the-planet" folks in this industry—she'll eventually meet with a good percentage of them.

I keep stating "letter" rather than e-mail...but it's all the same, right? Nope! Unless your target expert is someone you know personally, it is best to approach them in a formal letter rather than an e-mail.

Given the flood of e-mails we all receive daily, you don't want to be mentally associated with the angst of the inbox: the pervasive feeling that there are so many folks to get back to, so many items to address, and so on. The last thing you want is for your Approach Letter to end up buried under a bunch of other unresolved issues.

Plus, in a world of so much daily technological communication—e-mails, instant messages, social network posts and tweets, texts—a formal letter actually makes you stand out and be noticed. Think about it: Nobody sends letters anymore! So a physical letter actually makes itself known on someone's desk and must be dealt with, versus their busting-at-the-seams e-mail inbox.

Lastly, a formal letter is simply an elegant, old-world gesture that carries a bit of class with it if you do it correctly (proper grammar, spelling, punctuation, formatting—get a friend to check it!).

CareerGuy Tip: In today's technology-based communications world, to stand out, mail a letter.

A research-based stealth method takes time and effort, an organized approach, and follow-up. Such planned approaches net you more of what you seek in any area of life. The spaghetti approach of throwing it all against the wall (blasting out resumes and "I Need a Job!" cover letters all over creation) and seeing what sticks may be easier…but far less fruitful.

A traditional, overt approach might eventually get you a job, but at nowhere near the pace, salary, and informational value that operating stealth provides—and definitely nowhere near the enjoyment of exploration. Plus, through overt search, you end up in any job where someone says, "Okay then, I guess we'll hire you." Using a stealth approach, you avail yourself of roles and environments more truly aligned with who you are and what turns you on.

Principle #7: Eyes-to-Eyes Gets You the Prize

Your next task is to simply follow up on your Approach Letter in a timely way. That means: getting on the phone to set up a meeting with your target.

Always remember that your objective—from which you will be neither deterred nor misdirected—is to meet with your target experts personally: *NOT over the phone, by e-mail, or via a social network!* The phone, and other forms of technological communication, is an impersonal killer of effective relationship-building.

It's true that you may connect with people electronically initially, such as through mining your social network connections. But you want to transform that initial electronic contact into a personal, face-to-face one as quickly as possible…and you do so through the Approach Letter. (NOTE: *If*, and *only if*, you've already connected with someone via e-mail or through a social network, then you can e-mail your Approach Letter. If not, stick to the letter.)

 *CareerGuy Tip: Turn your online contacts to in-the-flesh contacts to create effective stealth relationships.*

A case could be made that you are conducting a research project that could legitimately be discussed over the phone. But, the ultimate objective of this method is to create and maintain relationships with people so that you are someone consistently known by the people in the know. You can't build something reliably long-term over the phone or by posting to a social network. It takes that face-to-face element to become truly embedded in people's minds.

Therefore, from the outset, get clear on the purpose of your follow-up calls to your Approach Letter recipients. It is not to get the answers to your research project! It is specifically and only to set a meeting!

Be ready for this, because once you reach your target, that person may helpfully suggest supplying the information you need right then and there, on the phone. Avoid that at all costs and go for setting the meeting.

Realize that there are certain nuances—and even chemical reactions—that human beings experience in face-to-face encounters that you don't want to miss, and you'll absolutely **need** these factors working for you to establish a long-term relationship.

THE MEETING SETUP

Here are seven guidelines to follow in setting up your face-to-face meetings:

1. Keep your word.

Call your targets at the time you specify in your Approach Letters ("I'll call your office next week") and, short of stalking, plan to keep following up until you speak to your target and set a meeting.

2. Ask to speak to your target, casually, and by first name.

Reach directly for the target ("Is Tom in?") but be prepared to get to know others in the process. If you're shooting high enough, you won't always reach your target directly the first time you try. You may need to connect with his assistant...or even with the dreaded main system voicemail.

If you do reach a main system voicemail, or the specific target's voicemail, a message as simple as, "Hi, this is Rita Researcher. I'm calling for Tom regarding some research I'm conducting. I sent in a letter and am following up. Please have him return my call at…" can generally get you a return call…at least from an assistant.

Notice that you don't say, "Hi, *my name is*…" because that's a dead giveaway that they have no obligation to know you. Make your follow-up call from the mindset that they *should* know you (because you sent in a letter) and with a focused intent to get the information you seek. This way of thinking will give confidence and poise to your message.

If you do speak to a gatekeeper (receptionist, administrative assistant, and so on), avoid getting into in-depth conversations and explanations as to why you're calling. They are good people doing their job, and *your job* is to get past them.

For instance, if Tom's assistant answers his line saying "Tom O'Malley's office. How can I help you?"—definitely do not say, "Hi, I sent a letter into Mr. O'Malley last week about some research I'm doing and I'm wondering if he received it and could set up a time to meet me?" Too much information way too quickly! You're just begging for interrogatories and gatekeeper nets to be thrown all over you!

This assistant is busy with a thousand things and, unless and until you call attention to yourself as someone outside of the ordinary rush of the day, she will oftentimes not notice you. "Hi, is Tom in?" or, even better, simply, "Is Tom in?" will get you way further down the road…especially if said in the casual, subdued way you would ask for your friend if another member of his family picked up the phone when you called his home.

NOTE: Make sure you've done a bit of research before you shorten Thomas to Tom, and don't assume Robert is Bob either. Calling them something nobody else calls them is a surefire way to call attention to yourself! Check the website, ask the receptionist, or just listen to how the assistant refers to her boss.

 *CareerGuy Tip: William isn't always Bill, Richard isn't always Dick, and Catherine isn't always Cathy.*

Sure, you may still get a "What's this call regarding?" from the assistant, to which you can *casually* respond, "Just following up on some research I contacted him about. Is he available to speak?" If you're relaxed and easy, either the simple initial question, "Is Tom in?" or the short answer may get you straight to Tom or at least his voicemail...and his voicemail is always way better than leaving a message with someone else, because he hears *your* voice and you start to become a real person for him.

3. Make friends along the way.

Get to know the assistant's name so that you can relate to her more personally now and in the future. If treated with respect and a bit of basic psychology, right-hand assistants can be your biggest helpers in reaching your target.

"I'm wondering if you can help me, [Assistant's Name]?" will go farther than trying to bulldoze or fib your way past her, which will bite you in the end. Never be rude or dismissive to a target's assistant (or anyone for that matter)! Never discount the sway she has with the boss when the boss doesn't know you from Adam!

4. Be truthful.

Again, if you're asked, "What is this regarding?" never say anything that could later be misinterpreted as untrue. The simple response, "Just following up on some research I contacted him about. Is he available to speak?" is true, and never say more if you don't need to.

If you've truly designed an authentic research project and are authentically seeking information, you'll always come out okay. If the assistant wants to dig in deeper, then you can go to another level in your answer, but always wait at each level of questioning before saying too much. Here's a simple scenario:

> Assistant: What research project?
>
> You: I'm doing a study of the new green technologies being applied in the Central Valley. Is he in today?
>
> Assistant: Exactly what is it you need?
>
> You: I sent in a letter last week describing my research. Do you know if he received it?
>
> Assistant: I don't remember that letter. Tell me more about what you need.
>
> You: You know, how about this—what's your name?
>
> Assistant: Mary.
>
> You: Okay, Mary, what if I send it again, and I could even address it to you? Would you be able to help me get it in front of him? I'm sure he's busy, but I am only asking for five to 10 minutes of his time. Should I e-mail or send it by postal mail again?

(Notice that you always offer a bit more information when requested, but then have an immediate follow-up question to get you closer to your goal.)

The conversation could go in many directions, but try to avoid getting into details over the phone because there's just too much room for misinterpretation. If the target or assistant is not familiar with your letter, don't try to explain its contents. Just offer to send it again. If she says, "Well, why don't you explain to me what you need," just respond politely that it's pretty detailed and you don't mind resending. What you lose in terms of a couple days you will more than gain back in terms of relationship-building.

If you try to explain the reason for the letter or its contents right then, in the moment, the assistant may make a quick assumption—before getting all the info that a *noninteractive* letter can give—that you want a job, and just cut you off or send you to HR. That's what you *don't want to happen!* If the assistant or target hasn't seen the letter, always quickly opt to send it again rather than explain.

5. Focus on a meeting, not immediate conversation.

When you speak directly with the target, or leave a voicemail, keep your conversation short of detail, and simply ask if she received your letter (never call it an Approach Letter!) and when she would be available to meet you for five to 10 minutes.

If the target asks for more detail, then be as authentic, friendly, and compelling in briefly describing your research project and asking, again, to meet for five to 10 minutes when he or she is least busy. If she wants to help you but tries to give you your research answers over the phone, refer to Point 6: Meet in the Office. Turn that conversation into a face-to-face meeting *whatever it takes!*

6. Meet in the Office

You want a face-to-face meeting, and you want it in your target's office. Your target will rarely suggest meeting outside of the office for coffee or a meal when she doesn't know you. That's great…because you don't want that!

Perhaps you've heard the phrases "never eat alone" or "take a millionaire to lunch"? These are great ideas for further developing a relationship once it has been established. But for many reasons, you want your first meeting to be in your target's place of work. Even if you are connecting with someone you already know but in a new way (as part of your research), you still want to have that first stealth meeting in her office. Here's why:

☞ You want your target operating in her business mind, not her relaxed and casual mind. When folks get out of the office, it's easy to put their professional world aside and kick back. Again, this is a good goal to have for the relationship down the road, but initially, you want your target thinking with a professional/business mind within her standard business setting—even if it's a *home office!*

☞ When having coffee or lunch, there are interruptions, wait staff running around, tabletops full of glasses and plates so you can't sit anything down, and so on. Your target's place of work, however, is a controlled setting in which your target is most comfortable and at home. True, there is the chance of work distractions, but you'll still come out better in the long run. Plus, you can better manage that environment in a specific way to produce the desired results of the meeting.

☞ You'll often be right next door to your targets' coworkers and, depending on how your contacts respond to your request for connections, it might be as simple as them walking you next door and introducing you to some of those coworkers.

☞ You're there to conduct research, not to get a job. However, it is always smart to get a sense of different work settings, organizational environments, and so on. Any time you can get an opportunity to explore different office and work settings, you expand your knowledge of the various options that exist in the world. It's good for research!

☞ Most importantly, meeting with your target in her place of work means she also has quick access to the contacts-management system…what we used to call a Rolodex. Following The 5 Stages of a Stealth Interview, you'll want your target to have ready access to those contacts. When you're out to lunch, your target doesn't always have those contacts on hand. Her PDA may have some, but having your target in close proximity to her e-mail database, files, and other business records is a smart move.

This point can't be emphasized enough: *Never, ever allow yourself to get sucked into conducting your stealth interview over the phone!* If you do, you will lose all the benefits, personal nuances, and even chemical reactions that occur when two people meet face to face.

If a targeted contact says, "I'm really busy. Let's just take a moment to talk now," your response should be, "I truly appreciate your time and need very little of it. However, I find there are certain elements to the information I am obtaining that I don't capture as well over the phone. Plus, I'm gaining so much additional value through the exposure to various environments. How about you tell me the absolute best time in your day when you could take only five to 10 minutes to chat with me and I'll drop by for a moment then." Keep asking for what you want and need.

7. Follow up, follow up, follow up.

Be persistent about fulfilling your research project. Continue to patiently check in with your target until you speak to her and set a meeting.

Often, people give up far too soon in reaching the people or objectives they have set for themselves. Look folks: people are *busy!* Just because they haven't responded to you yet doesn't mean they wouldn't be interested in talking to you. They've just got a lot on their plates. A patient, steady, and undauntable persistence often pays off. You have to press past ideas of rejection or being a bother and, unless and until you connect, keep focused and dedicated to gaining the information and relationship you desire.

CareerGuy Tip: If you fail to keep asking, the no is assured.

Here's a story that proves the point. A client once wanted to move from her role in sales and account management for a graphic design firm into a hands-on graphic design position within the entertainment industry—specifically in the design of DVD packaging for home video. She was working full time, but she built her stealth campaign into her already full life.

For her research, she focused on senior executives in the Hollywood movie studios. One of her approach letters was sent to the VP of home video for a certain studio. She re-sent the same letter for several months, one after another, befriending the administrative assistant, leaving a voicemail every couple weeks, and simply showing no signs of stopping her patient, yet relentless pursuit of her research project. (Of course, prodding and encouragement from me, after her initial tendency to give up, helped a bit.)

She consistently left messages for the target through the assistant and made each bi-monthly call such a fun and play-ful game of "catch the target" that she enrolled the assistant in playing with her! "Oh, darn, you just missed her...but I did give her the message from last week!"

Four months later, she received a call from her target con-tact, apologizing profusely, saying how guilty she felt that she had never been able to call back because of simply being too busy. My client's patient, yet persistent behavior gave her brownie points in the end—the VP was apologizing to *her*! Of course, she did not make the VP wrong, but deftly used the apologetic energy as an inroad to schedule a meeting for the following week. She capitalized on the relationship eq-uity she had built up by getting to meet the VP for an ex-tended period of time...*and* even found a way to get the VP's opinion on her full portfolio!

Not all stealth campaigns take months but, when you're working full time, the steady and plodding ability to expand the world's awareness of you is priceless...and worth it. This is a perfect example of how patient, upbeat, relentless determination can pay off in a big way.

I want to focus a bit more on staying away from casual settings for the first meeting. This advice applies even more strongly if you're setting up meetings with people you already know, because they will *especially* want to chew the fat over what's been happening in your respective lives, families, and so on.

Lunch and dinner meetings are great opportunities to get to know someone better on a personal level, or to enjoy an already existing personal relationship. Once again, this is smart in building or maintaining long-lasting relationships *after the initial stealth research meeting*. Just make sure you engage in this more casual networking only *after* you've accomplished your interview objectives in a formal setting: the target's office. If a long-term acquaintance suggests meeting over lunch, agree that you'd love to have lunch *and* you would receive much greater benefit if you can do so *after* meeting him in his office.

CareerGuy Tip: For stealth purposes, meet friends and family where they work to shake up the old ways of relating to them.

Realize that you are conducting a professional career exploration campaign, so you want to call on the *professional* side of your personal contacts. Though it may initially seem unusual to approach them strictly professionally, these people often have a "business world" life that you may be insufficiently aware of. So, for these individuals in particular, as well as all others that you'll approach completely "cold," you always want the environment to be strictly about business.

To address the obvious weirdness in contacting your current relationships in such a formal way, I advocate using a first-paragraph "disclaimer" at the top of the Approach Letter. For example, let's say you actually knew Thomas O'Malley. You'd simply add a weirdness-reducing section to the top of the standard Approach Letter format.

Close Relationship Approach Letter

Thomas O'Malley, Chief Engineer
EcoFan, Inc.
11467 Hillcrest Drive
High Pointe, OR 97031

Dear Thomas,
I know this may seem a very formal approach given our long relationship. However, I write specifically for two reasons. First, in beginning a systematic industry research campaign, I believe there may be knowledge and information you have that I'm not already aware of and, in this way, I want to open up a different kind of dialogue between us. Second, frankly, I am just beginning a very structured way of conducting my campaign and need a guinea pig on whom to practice my approach. Please bear with me.
I am writing to you because of your unique position within the renewable energy industry. I have observed the development of EcoFan as a significant player within the wind energy

field, and am particularly fascinated by the new technologies being adapted to wind turbines in the Central Valley.

Frankly, I don't know as much as I'd like about the direction wind energy is headed in the Pacific Northwest, which is why I'm seeking information. I'm particularly researching the engineering requirements for municipalities to take advantage of these growing technologies.

Because of your senior role as a leader within this burgeoning field, I thought you might be able to give me some information regarding my research. Please be aware, I don't expect you to have a job or to know of any. However, 5 minutes of your time would be most helpful as I gather information on the subject.

Hoping you could offer me five minutes of your time when most convenient for you, I'll call your office in the next week to schedule an appointment. I have enclosed my pertinent information, just so you have a sense of my background.

Sincerely,
Steve Stealth

Notice that everything after the first paragraph is the same as Rita Researcher's letter before. After the initial disclaimer, you want to use the same basic approach because it is this different kind of conversation you will conduct with him that will net you different outcomes. You'll get information and contacts who have always been right at your fingertips if you had only known how to tap into them effectively.

As mentioned, most people's approach to those they (think they) know well goes as far as, "Hey, I got laid off. Let me know if you hear of anything"…which generally gets them nowhere. But realize that it's critical to have a real re-search project even with people you've known, for it is this unique way of interacting with them that creates results beyond the inept standard method of asking for "anything."

 CareerGuy Tip: Be careful when asking to hear of "anything" because you just might get it!

Principle #8: Building Relationship Equity...One Meeting at a Time

The job now is simple: to meet face to face with as many "experts" as possible in your fields of interest and to begin stockpiling information and relationships. Following up on your Approach Letters skillfully will net you meetings, and the more you practice those follow-ups and meetings, the better you'll get at the whole process.

There are four steps for the preparation and conduct of an effective stealth meeting.

Step 1: The first step is, as you know, the Approach Letter you sent. Ideally, it is based on a creatively designed research project in which your target—someone you already know or someone new—is the expert and has unique information to offer you.

Step 2: The second step is to follow up on your Approach and set the face-to-face meeting.

Step 3: The third step is to create 20 questions to ask them about your research project. That's easy: If you are really discussing something you're passionate about, it won't be hard to come up with questions about the subject. Refer back to the exercises you did in Principle #3 to discover what you are truly passionate about. Create a list of 20 questions that this person could provide insight on to help your exploration of that area. You'll hardly ever ask those questions point blank, but you want to clearly have in your mind the areas in which this specific person could be of most informational insight before you go into your meeting.

As described earlier, the questions could range from very technical or future growth matters concerning an industry you already know about and in which you can hold the interviewee up as an expert. Or, perhaps you design questions about a new field of interest or fascination, in which you hold this interviewee as simply a "smart person" from whom you could get input.

Whatever the approach, you want to have a specific reason why this particular person can offer you unique advice and direction…and to construct questions along those lines. Write them down and bring them with you—along with a copy of the "pertinent information" (resume) that you included with the Approach Letter—inside a folding portfolio that you can flip open to take notes.

Step 4: The fourth step is to conduct the meeting following the The 5 Stages of a Stealth Interview.

It is critical to the success of your interviews that you organize and run your meetings to provide you with exactly what you came for: information, input, advice, a personal connection, referrals, and so on. You'll never actually use the terms "stealth interview" or "referrals" in the conversations themselves—those are terms used only for teaching purposes. While engaging in this process, be clear that *you* are the interviewer and you will be sitting down with *your* interviewees. In this way, you are controlling the process yourself, which allows many more possibilities to arise than in a standard conversation or traditional, overt job interview.

THE 5 STAGES OF A STEALTH INTERVIEW

Stage 1: Acknowledgment and bonding

This first stage is the most important opportunity to establish rapport and relationship. Remember, first impressions are everything! The first several seconds of a meeting can greatly influence the character of your entire time together. Therefore, you want to point the attention of these first moments toward that area most likely to receive favorable response: the interviewee. What one thing do people most enjoy talking about? Themselves! So, you want to focus first on them, and use your authentic interest to begin obtaining the information you need.

EXAMPLE: While in the process of sitting down in the interviewee's office, or even on the way to the office during the initial handshake, you want to deliver a statement such as this: "First off, let me thank you for giving me the opportunity to chat with you. I appreciate that your time is important and I have a list of questions in areas I'd love to explore with you. But first, before we even get started, if I could take a moment, I'd just love to know how you got here. Where were you before this? Why did you choose this industry or company? What background enabled you to get into such a position?"

It doesn't matter what you initially ask, just make sure it's something that will get this person talking about herself. I've stated several times throughout the book that it's always better to be interested than interesting. You'll notice, if you just probe a person and her professional life by being very interested, moving from one naturally occurring question to another, that you will probably get many of the questions on your list answered without even looking at it. (That's why you prepare the questions and know them inside and out beforehand…so you don't need to look at them!) Better yet, you'll get those questions answered from their experience rather than just a cold list of Q & As…which could be over in a matter of minutes.

The idea here is to truly inquire and truly listen to this person's journey, not to operate as some reporter or investigator, impersonally running through questions. You want to be present with this person and have her feel that what she has to say is truly special. In doing so, you accomplish several objectives:

☞ You obtain the information you seek: knowledge and experience that will help you in your direction.

☞ You allow the interviewee to extol her personal path, choices, values, and virtues. People want to justify and validate their lives, and there's rarely the opportunity to find interested listeners who treat them like experts in their own workplace. This is truly a subconscious gift you are bestowing upon them! Someone is interested in their thoughts, their opinions, and their life path. This is golden in terms of building up your relationship equity.

☞ The interviewee subconsciously ascribes a certain amount of intelligence to you just by the act of your listening, even if she knows nothing yet about you. Think about it: you're smart enough to listen to her!

☞ You also create a subconscious sense of being beholden to you. When you've really listened, an inner desire to be of some assistance to you grows. It's just human nature: If you give a lot to me, I'm going to be thinking, "What can I do for you?" Fact is, you're just simply more liked in life when your focus is on being interested rather than interesting.

 **CareerGuy Tip: *You're always more liked by listening.***

Stage 2: Questions

Again, focus on getting as many answers to your questions while you're discussing their background. This is how you get the specific information you need. By being interested rather than interesting, you're building strong relationship equity to cash in later.

The truth is, the long-range value of your meeting will always come more from the development of an actual relationship with your target than from the relative value of any particular question you could ask. That's not to say to leave out those burning, authentically fascinated questions you have…but know that the main purpose of this first contact is to establish an ongoing relationship that gets *all* your questions *always* answered by a new friend!

The simple act of showing genuine interest in Stage 1 will very well take you beyond the initial five to 10 minutes requested for the interview because you want to have this person talk about herself as much as possible. If you've asked probing questions and really milked this person's sharing as much as possible, you will often find yourself 30 minutes into the meeting still talking about her! This is good!

Remember, you started the whole conversation with this phrase, which is crucial: "But first, before we even get started, if I could take a moment, I'd just love to know…." You said that because you wanted to distinguish this initial conversation as preceding the one you came in for, even though this is exactly what you came in for.

As 20 to 30 minutes may now have passed, for the sake of integrity, you need to at least acknowledge that you've gone over and request a few minutes. If you've established good rapport, this shouldn't be a problem.

EXAMPLE: [Look at your watch] "Wow! Oh my gosh, I so appreciate your taking the time to walk me through your own path of success. It's really inspiring, and you've already answered many of my questions. I do notice that we've gone over the five to 10 minutes I requested. Is it alright if I have just a couple more minutes to ask you a last question or two that I had prepared?"

You've built up so much relationship equity at this point that she will agree to give you a few more minutes. There will likely be no hesitation whatsoever on her part because she feels inwardly honored by your interest in her. You have no idea of how gifted people feel when being listened to and what they are then willing to do for you, until you try this!

Then, simply review your list of questions, seeing if there's anything burning that wasn't covered. Don't ask more than one more from the list (if any), because you want your very last question to be the Resume Slip.

Stage 3: The Resume Slip

As your last question, you'll take out your resume and place it on the desk, facing the person, asking, "Just one last question. Can you do me a favor? I'm going to shut up for a couple minutes. Would you take a look at this and tell me X?"

Your "X" can be one of many things: "...if I were to choose to go this direction one day, what parts of my background would fit into the field we've been discussing?" "... as part of my research, I've been wondering how my experience relates to this industry. What do you see that would be relevant if I were to focus more in this area?" "...as part of my research, and determining a possible congruence to this field, what do you see that I should emphasize more or less if I were to connect with others in this area?"

Again, the particular question doesn't matter as long as you ask something that gets her quietly reviewing your background. The idea is to first set her up for a bit of "quiet time" ("I'm going to shut up for a couple minutes...") and then to ask a question that causes your contact to delve deeply into the resume. She received it when you sent it with your Approach Letter...but likely didn't read it.

One caveat: what is critical in the design of your Resume Slip question is that it be absolutely congruent with the overall research that you're doing, not some shifty "Okay, now let's talk about me and getting a job!!" That incongruence will throw everything off, and both you and your interviewee will feel weird. Yes, in the end, you'll eventually land an opportunity out of your research, contacts, relationships, and so on, but you need to always remember the research mode that those interactions need to be conducted within… and the Resume Slip question you ask must relate specifically to that research.

Notice that you didn't use the word *resume* but rather *this*. You don't want to shift into a job-search mindset by using the "r" word. Just as you referred to it as your pertinent information in the Approach Letter, simply put it in front of her and refer to it indirectly.

CareerGuy Tip: In stealth meetings, stay in research mode, at all times, under all circumstances.

This particular stage is where outright magic can occur because of the relationship equity you've built up in your bank account. Because you were interested in her and her story earlier, she will feel compelled to answer this last question. This is why you don't want to ask many more questions before this one because you want to capitalize right away on that built-up equity/energy.

Several results may occur from her reviewing your background to answer your Resume Slip question:

☞ At a minimum, she could give you valuable feed-back and simply answer your inquiry, which is enormously helpful in its own right.

☞ She may notice something in your background that could stir a memory of a position that either she or someone she knows may have available, or a particular direction you might pursue.

☞ She might notice something about you that will trigger someone or something she knows that could net you more information or contacts to help you.

In any of these ways, you win because you have now just completely bypassed Human Resources in order to get your detailed background in front of an influential player who knows other influential players, playgrounds, and opportunities to play!

Stage 4: Request for connections

This is where your web of networking begins. A referral from one person to another, if a substantial relationship exists between them, is often a sure bet in terms of another stealth interview. Therefore, you need to be very clear that you have truly appreciated this person's help and would be extremely grateful for any names of others who might give you guidance in a similar way.

Just as you don't use the term *resume*, never use the terms *referral* or *contacts*, but rather, *others who can be as helpful as you have been*. Also, make sure that your request for others to speak to is specifically about your research project—not anything to do with "looking for a job." You must stay focused in your approach…because people smell insincerity.

"Your input has been extremely valuable to me as I continue to gather information on this subject. Do you know of others who can be as helpful as you have been with whom I could speak?"

Wait for her to think. If she gives you a few names, jot them down with numbers and e-mail/mailing addresses, if possible. If she can't think of anyone at the moment, assure her that you don't mean to put her on the spot and, if she would be willing to think about it for a day or so, you will call back to see if anyone comes to mind. Give a specific time you'll follow up, such as, "Okay, no problem. I know there might not be names on the tip of your tongue. Would you mind thinking about it a bit and perhaps I can give you a call on Monday at 10 a.m. and see if you've thought of anyone?"

On average, you'll get two to three referrals from each person. Some might give you six. Others might not give you any. In time, you will receive ample referrals to allow you to build up an exponentially growing group of relationships.

NOTE: If anyone ever offers to "pass your information along" to someone else, thank them profusely for that willingness, but do all you can to be in control of that contact process. "I really appreciate your willingness to help me connect with others, but I know your time is valuable. You probably have a lot of things on your plate right now. What if, to make it easier for you, I contact them directly and copy you on it? That way, you don't have to be the middleman, but they will still see our connection. Would that work for you? Of course, any heads up you could give them about me is also greatly appreciated, but this way you don't have to worry yourself with follow-ups and such."

An alternative is to ask if he can do an e-mail introduction for you, in which he e-mails the person but copies you. Either way, the idea is for you to be in control of your campaign process and not to be "commoditized" by having your resume just floating out there. People will never get the full essence of you from your resume that they will get from a personal Approach Letter and direct contact with you, so try to always be the one in control of that process while definitely utilizing the name of the referring party.

Stage 5: Thank-you

Be sure to acknowledge the interviewee again for his or her time and help. Provide a card with your number and e-mail on it and say, "Again, thank you so much for your time and input. I'm only in the beginning stages of my research and, if it's alright, I'd love to follow up with you if another question arises…or, perhaps, just to keep you posted on my progress. Is that alright?" She will say, "Sure, absolutely!" Then, get her e-mail address if you don't already have it.

 **CareerGuy Tip: Just because you don't have a job doesn't mean you shouldn't have a business card. Get one for your search!**

Immediately send this person a thank-you e-mail or letter acknowledging the time she spent with you as well as the specific information she offered. After that, you need to find a reason to keep in touch with this person on a regular basis, in some way or another, for the rest of your career.

Wait! Did you read that right? *For the rest of your career?* Yes! This person has now unknowingly become someone you will ingratiate yourself into the consciousness of for as long as you need a career tribe. This isn't a one-shot deal; this is about building a network for life!

During the campaign process itself, if you're currently unemployed, you'll leave a follow-up voicemail or send a follow-up e-mail every 30 days (a sample follows). Once you have secured your next opportunity, or if you are currently employed, you'll do follow-ups every 90 days, unless you want to follow up sooner. But a definite systematic structure of follow-up is crucial to developing your career tribe. Forever.

These are the stages you want to follow in every stealth meeting. There is an art and science to it...and you'll see in time that it works. It *really* works! As you master this process, soon you'll have so much activity that the sheer numbers involved will generate opportunities left and right.

You might ask: "If I keep it only focused on research and stay true to my word, why will she ever turn me on to opportunities?" Because you're interested in the subject, and she has an initial and soon-to-be ongoing basis to like you and think of you!

Remember, you never need to say, "I need a job!" You've shown interest in this person and what she is interested in. You've asked probing questions. You've inquired as to how your background might apply, were you to go the direction of your research (the Resume Slip). And you've established an ongoing relationship by asking if you can stay connected. In time, by merely doing what you said—staying connected—you'll be top-of-mind whenever relevant news or opportunities arise.

But more importantly, you want to realize that the magic of this process lies not only in the establishment of a relationship with this particular individual, but, in the formation of relationships with the literally tens, hundreds, or thousands of individuals that lie *behind* this person. Through the many Internet social networks that folks utilize today, some professional and some personal, you get a true glimpse of how one person connects you with many. In this process, you're simply operating off of that same concept, *but in person…where the deeper, chemical bonds of relationship can be formed.*

So, remember that behind every individual you meet, there are an infinite number of additional contacts for you to mine for more information and to establish more relationships. You'll simply start the whole process over again with each of them: Approach Letter (mentioning your referrer), follow up, and stealth meeting (following the same five stages). It becomes exponential. You begin to form your own career tribe.

Principle # 9: Top-of-Mind Is Easy to Find

The key to leveraging the initial stealth meeting into a relationship for life is staying connected. You've opened the door. Now, you just need to keep it open.

In Stage 5, you set yourself up to be in regular contact after your stealth interview, and you want to do just that. Never build up an awesome career tribe only to drop it and let it wither away once you land a job somewhere. For sure, you need to keep it vibrant and active while you're still in search mode. But you want to maintain it even after you land your next opportunity—because there will always be another transition down the road.

There are many ways to stay connected. For instance, you might see an article that would interest one of your career tribe members and forward it to him along with a note. Or, you might give him a call once a month to update him on your progress while in your stealth campaign...and then every three to four months after you've landed a job. By far, however, the most effective way I've taught people to maintain relationships is by sending what I call Holiday Letters.

You've received holiday letters, haven't you? You know, during the end-of-year holiday season when your mailbox gets filled with cards, out of which fall folded letters giving you the rundown on everything that happened in these people's lives during the last year. "This was a very full year for the Schmoe family. Little Joey fell off his bike in July, and Cindy became a school cheerleader in September..." On and on they go, telling you every little event that occurred for the past 12 months.

You want to use that same principle for ongoing contact with your career tribe members. While you're actively working your stealth campaign, you'll send a more engaging version of a Holiday Letter by e-mail every 30 days to the folks with whom you've had stealth meetings. An example might be:

From: Rita Researcher

Sent: Friday, September 28, 2012

To: Thomas o'Malley [thomas.omalley@ecofan.com]

Subject: Follow-up

Hi Thomas,

I'm writing to touch base and follow up on our meeting two months ago. As I mentioned in my e-mail last month, your insight really set me on a great path of research.

If you remember, you suggested that I speak with Denise Hutchinson on the City of Portland's Renewable Energy Task Force. She had been out of town, but I finally met with her last week.

It was, indeed, a worthwhile contact, as she was able to inform me of the factors involved in determining the wind component of the Task Force's research, as well as connect me with several of the main players in conversation with the city. I'll be following up with those individuals soon.

Also, I did some further research into the role of "engineering intermediaries" who serve as liaisons between municipalities and turbine providers. I spoke with a few folks who have consulted in those roles and even ran into Fred Davis, who said he knew you.

I just wanted to keep you apprised of my efforts and say thanks again for the direction you provided. If you think of any other avenues I should pursue or other folks I should speak to, please let me know.

Also, if you're available, I'd like to take you for coffee or lunch next month and discuss more fully all that I'm finding out. I'll call your office in a few weeks to see what would work for you.

Sincerely,

Rita Researcher

Every month, like clockwork, you send updates such as this, informing them of everything that has transpired since your last communication...and asking them to keep you informed if they think of other research prospects. If you really work this program, during the course of a month of activities, something else has taken place: you've had more meetings, gained further insight, or obtained more information. Like a monthly episodic soap opera, you are pulling them in and ingratiating yourself into their consciousness by simply updating them.

Sending an e-mail beats calling on the phone every month because they might not have time to talk when you call, and you don't want unanswered messages piling up on their desk or in voicemail. Plus, you don't get to share as much in a voicemail. An e-mailed Holiday Letter plants the top-of-mind "heads up" you want in their awareness, yet updates them on your story on their time schedule.

Whether you hear back from these regular missives or not doesn't matter; the point is that, by sending them, you stay top-of-mind. It's like advertising: You hear about the same product every day on TV, or see the same retailer in every issue of such-and-such magazine. Being top-of-mind allows them to remember you when something of interest to you comes into their world. It could be a specific opportunity. It might be a piece of information or newsflash that could help you. Or it might be another person they meet who could be a resource for you. You never know what is going to come into their world after you leave them…but you *want to know* if it's related to your topic.

CareerGuy Tip: To stay abreast of all that relevant info that your contacts hear about after you leave them, just never really leave them.

So, you seed and nurture them with an ongoing awareness of you. Like clockwork. They then contact you about the information and opportunities that can help you. It's just the way human beings are built: They become alert and triggers go off in their brain when information that has been planted as being important—to them or to someone else—comes up.

Notice in the Holiday Letter, a few months into the relationship, you take it outside of the office to further establish an ongoing feeling of collegiality with them. My clients have said that when they reconnect face to face with contacts a few months later in a more casual setting, they generally get *even more referrals* than they did during the first stealth interview. It makes sense, because your targets now feel more connected with you and, therefore, begin opening up their lifetime of connections even wider. You've carved out a greater residence within their conscious minds.

Besides establishing immediate relationships that will help you land your next position, an ongoing, well-managed career tribe with antennae out in the marketplace can assist you in securing your subsequent position, and the next one, and the next one. Don't get so submerged in your new job that you let your career tribe fall apart. The worst mistake you can make is to cut off your connection with the network you've developed.

Though giving fully to your new employer or situation, always keep 10 percent or more of *you* reserved for *your* long-term security by maintaining your career tribe. Keep it alive and vital and it will ensure that you never get caught again with your career pants down. Through your vibrant career tribe, you will often hear about your next great career opportunity long before you're finished with the current one!

 *CareerGuy Tip: Fight the urge to submerge when you land your new role.*

Here are the pipelines necessary to initiate, run, manage, and maintain an effective stealth campaign for career tribe development. You want to fill up each of them sequentially and then keep the flow going through all. Never stop the first one, as it initiates all the rest.

1. **Approach Letters going out:** Never stop researching potential contacts in your areas of passionate interest, even after you've landed in a position. There's always more information and knowledge to gain through research projects, and additional contacts only add to your lifetime career tribe security.

2. **Follow-ups on letters sent:** This is simply part of the process of moving toward the face-to-face meeting, which is your ultimate objective. Your follow-ups must be timely and, as described earlier, will become increasingly effective in netting you meetings when you practice, practice, practice.

3. **Conduct your stealth interviews:** Following The 5 Stages of a Stealth Interview, hold your meetings, gain valuable information, receive helpful referrals, and establish wonderful ongoing connection, with your targeted experts.

4. **Thank-you and Holiday Letters:** Send immediate thanks for the valuable information and referrals gained from your meetings, and follow up every 30 days with a Holiday Letter updating your career tribe member with your progress, the information you've gained, the advice you've followed, and your ongoing status of openness for

additional information and connections. After you land a job, these Holiday Letters are sent every three to four months with an update on your career in general, the paths you're pursuing, the projects you're involved with, and your open willingness to support your career tribe member in any way.

5. **Repeat, repeat, repeat:** Take every referral obtained and every new target discovered through these same steps. Keep the process going...and watch your world of opportunities expand beyond your imagination.

NOTE: Resources for managing your contacts as well as your overall stealth campaign are available at *www.careerguy. com/campaign.*

Principle # 10: Treat Yourself Like a Business to Stay in Business

Learning effective relationship development and management is critical when you need a job immediately. But mastering these techniques and utilizing them as a lifetime career management practice during the course of your entire career is a whole different matter.

A mindset shift to step into is that of being a business owner, even if you've only ever considered yourself an employee. Consider that you have always had your own business and that you've merely chosen to lease your employable assets out to particular companies. Yes, those lease arrangements may have been for years at a time, but they were lease arrangements, nonetheless.

If you had a 20-foot trailer in your backyard and you made a side income from renting it to folks to haul things, you'd want to rent it to those who would pay you the most, correct? Even if it were leased out on a month-to-month agreement for a few years to one particular user, if you found out that another user would pay you double the rental rate, you'd rent it to the new person, right?

Similarly, you want to keep attuned to your ROI (Return on Individuality) or ROE (Return on Effort) of the employable assets that you lease out to employers. They are only "employers" because they employ *your* assets for *their* use. But, they are *your* assets.

Think like a business owner: you want to make sure you are always getting the most return for those employable assets. It may be the amount of salary you receive, it could be the type of work you engage in, or it might be the particular environment you become a part of…but there are various ways in which you receive a return on your assets.

 *CareerGuy Tip: Your own business's viability measures: ROI = Return on Individuality, ROE = Return on Effort.*

It's smart business to always know about your other investment options so that you steward your assets for the highest return. If this book is the first time you've really considered the value of effective career relationship development, good for you. The time is now to begin building those muscles.

When you begin going to the gym, those muscles, skills, and abilities will grow through exertion and expansion in time…*if* you regularly practice. Whether you're new to the gym of career networking or not, realize that it is simply good business to always have your finger on the pulse of the market and the cornucopia of investment options available. So get and stay connected! Use the principles outlined in this book to both build your career tribe and maintain it for the rest of your working life. Lifetime career management is smart business. Again, "You can pay me now, or you can pay me later." Find the time in your schedule, utilize all the social networking tools available today, but most importantly, employ the personalized follow-up methods to keep vital connections in place. That way, you don't have to start over in building contacts every time a job change hits you unawares. The small effort and time you invest regularly in maintaining your career tribe relationships can pay big dividends when you least expect it.

Conclusion

In the Preface, I asked you to provide the little bit extra that makes a world of difference by putting something at stake for yourself in fully engaging in this book. Did you fully engage? Did you complete the exercises? Did you launch and begin working your stealth campaign? If so, I would love to hear from you and learn about the results you've produced. Do you see the possibility of fulfilling what you put at stake as you continue along this path of relationship development?

What is possible here, as has been demonstrated by the many stories of stealth breakthroughs throughout this book, is a breakthrough for you, too. It does take some initial understanding, development, and practice. But it gets easier with time and becomes just another part of life. And the results of *even one powerful new relationship that opens up a new possibility for you* is completely worth it, because your whole career can shift due to one new contact.

If you choose to review this book and its method from the beginning, take a moment to go back right now and review Miracle Moves #1 and #2 in Chapter 2 and note, again, the six major points to pull from those stories.

Remember that both Eileen and Jim not only utilized the stealth method of networking, but both had the advantage of having built up their self-esteem by a thorough **career-inventory process**...which then led to a **unique and distinguishing "personal brand."** For some folks, those initial steps can provide the renewed inspiration and sense of self-worth and individuality that make what may seem a bold process of developing a career tribe through a stealth campaign more conceivable. You can do *everything right* and "by the book" as outlined here, but if your *inner* game isn't as up to speed with your *outer* game, your results may be less fruitful. You always attract opportunities more by what you feel and believe than what you "do." Be sure to find ways to gain an awareness of how exceptionally unique and awesome you are. That awareness, along with this method, will make you very attractive.

For more resources to support your career growth and development, including that *inner game*, visit *www.careerguy.com*. You'll find free tools to assist you in many of the exercises and processes outlined in this book, along with audios, eBooks, and transformational programs to support your career efforts.

Also, as a ritual full of pomp and circumstance to acknowledge the completion of your project to engage in and employ this new method, please download your free "Relationships Well Drilling Rights" certificate from *www.careerguy.com* right away.

In alignment with the principle of Harvey Mackay's bestselling book title, *Dig Your Well Before You're Thirsty*, you have now graduated into a never-ending lifetime career management practice of finding and digging your wells to ensure your most fulfilling career.

Appendix A: The Stealth Method in Action

In order to provide some inspiration and motivation for the task of establishing your own stealth campaign and career management process, as well as to demonstrate what arises from this approach compared to traditional, overt methods, I've included just a few stories from the many folks utilizing these techniques. More stories and experiences can be obtained at *www.careerguy.com/darrell-gurney-reviews/reviews.*

STEALTH CAREER 2.0

I was a quiet engineer who had spent the previous 18 years in operations and engineering environments. I was reasonably comfortable within the company walls, but had never really done any of this networking thing. I knew exactly where I was and what my strong points were. I didn't really need help, but a "stealth" approach sounded interesting.

So, I started the networking process somewhat tentatively. Now I am a total convert, having done more than 50 stealth meetings with an incredible variety of people, industries, and companies in my last campaign. The contacts and people I talked to were totally more than I could have ever dreamt of before learning this method. It really energized me!

During my campaign, I conducted one meeting at a restaurant (never the best environment) with a person whom I thought was a no-hoper. He referred me to a consultant, and, later, a half-hour discussion with this consultant changed my life. I suddenly realized that most of my requirements for truly passionate work were met by being a business consultant. "Ah-ha!" Maybe this is what I had always wanted to do, but never knew. And I still wouldn't know, nor have had that realization, sitting in front of the computer looking for a job. It was being out talking to people that gave me the insight I needed.

As I continue to network in this stealth way as a standard part of life, the leads that come in are incredible. I just got an opportunity to look at a vice president of operations position in an exclusive startup with incredible potential. How? Well, I followed up monthly with all the people I met with, using my personalized "holiday letters," letting them know where I was and what I was finding out. This kept me at the front of one particular person's mind. When a recruiter called him asking for leads to professionals who might fit the role, he immediately thought of me and gave me a glowing reference.

It takes a bit of effort to keep following up, but it is really worth that effort. Even if I only get a few replies, consistent "information updating" really works because, as has happened so many times, one day there is a match.

This has been an incredible experience and one that is launching me off into Career 2.0. Now I decide where and what I do, not an employer.

Peter Thompson

Consultant

www.streamlinedstrategies.com

Launching a New Career Using the Stealth Method

After 12 years as a senior manager in the hardware technology industry, I made the decision to explore other career opportunities.

I had five criteria for the new opportunity I was seeking:

1. Software not hardware

2. Under 100 employees

3. Less than 5 years old

4. Web 2.0 driven

5. Leadership role

The problem was: I had a hardware background with a large company. Add to it that I had not actively looked for a job in 20 years. Then I happened upon the stealth method.

I have to admit I thought it was a little crazy, but Darrell's confidence in the stealth method had me intrigued. As a salesperson, I knew that originality worked, but these are things that I would never have done before.

By diving into the process, I put together a detailed strategy of three formal meetings a week to gather information and ideas and specifically *not* to interview. I was amazed at how many business leaders were willing to spend time with me when I was not asking for a job. As a matter of fact, I had to really convince them at times that I really just wanted information. The education I gained during this process was priceless.

My face-to-face presentation skills were improving with each meeting. Usually only getting face to face during a typical job interview, there wasn't much opportunity to practice…because those came along only so often. But now that I was the one setting up interviews, I became more relaxed in just being with people outside of the typical interview anxiety…and it spread to all areas of my relationships. No pressure, just questions and conversation.

I was also getting referrals and being referred by people. The stealth approach is effective because folks do not feel apprehensive because you are not directly looking for a job.

With this method, I was actually able to find the perfect opportunity that fit all of my criteria. Keep in mind, this was spring of 2009, and not the best time for most people in making a career transition. But, it turned out to be the perfect time for me.

Three years later, I lead the third fastest-growing company in Austin, Texas, with annual growth of 175 percent. We were 663 on the Fortune 5000 Fastest-Growing E-commerce companies in the world. Starting with only five employees two years ago, we now have 40 with plans to expand to 200!

Folks ask me all the time how I got so lucky, how I was able to find the perfect opportunity and make such a huge industry shift in a down market. I tell them a good background, a good plan, and a good stealth approach!

Lee Sellers

Global Sales Manager

Interspire and Big Commerce

www.interspire.com

AN INTERNAL STEALTH MANEUVER

While coming to the end of a consulting engagement with Southern California Edison, I was working with Darrell to apply his stealth search techniques to find a full-time opportunity.

At the time, I actually had a job offer on the table from Accenture, which came as a result of a relationship I built with them during my engagement at SCE. In addition, the company I had worked for previously (NCR) had reached out to me about rejoining them.

All of these would have put me back on a plane essentially full-time again, which I was not excited about. However, while I had talked to the friend who had brought me into SCE about opportunities within his organization, he really had not structured a job specifically for me, nor actually created a full-time position. To make things more challenging, I did not know the industry that well and figured, even though they had engaged me as a consultant to manage a specific project, I really did not have the necessary knowledge to work in the industry.

However, as I worked on designing a career campaign, I began thinking about why I felt this way and why my skills could not apply at SCE *if* I was able to structure the right job. I began to ponder how to leverage the knowledge I was learning to open discussions with SCE. In effect, what I did was use the stealth method internally and started talking to people to understand how I might bring value to the company. It wasn't about interviewing for a job—because there wasn't one—but based on the stealth kind of meetings we were discussing at the time.

I ended up using the relationship-building skills to speak with a broad range of people at all levels within SCE: some junior, some peers, and some much more senior than I had been working with. Through these conversations, I was able to gain enough knowledge to both realize and articulate how my experience could actually be valuable in the right position, and then described that position in such a way that it would fit into the framework of SCE. In the vernacular of the company, it would be called a strategic planning manager.

So, even though I had other offers, which would have been a path of less resistance to take, I used the stealth method to actually design, create, and propose a new position within SCE. The entire process of this internal stealth campaign took six months. In the end, the company created a senior position specifically for me. The outcome was a job offer for a position I had crafted myself, including the level and compensation.

It still amazes me that I was able to accomplish this when SCE was in a completely different industry from the industry in which I had almost 30 years of career experience.

David Bartholomew
Strategic Planning Manager
Southern California Edison
Author of *The Diamond Principle*
www.thediamondprinciple.com

NON-PROFIT NETWORKING: TREADING BACK IN AND OUT VIA STEALTH MEANS

A few years ago, I had a position as a program director within a non-profit organization matching volunteers with isolated seniors. My daughters were quite young at the time, and the hours and flexibility of this job worked well with my girls' schedule.

Eventually, as a proud-yet-stretched-thin member of the sandwich generation, I had to take a hiatus to coordinate care for my mother. After a while, another time-limited project came and went. My girls were getting older, and I needed a full-time gig.

I had remained very close with my supervisor from the first job, and shared with her my vision of my ideal job. I had learned, through my adopting of a stealth method of career transition, that it was the channel of people that would lead me to my next right opportunity. So I made a point to share what I was really passionate about so she could be an educated antenna for me.

I was stealth networking with whomever I could think of, but I sensed that due to this former supervisor's position, intuitiveness, and acute listening skills, there was a good chance she would hear of something that would fit my ideal.

Sure enough, she called me one day not long after that and announced that there was a position about to be posted by the non-profit agency, and I needed to pounce. She simply stated "It's your job, Dawn!" I faxed my resume and cover letter, and immediately got a call.

Before I knew it, I was interviewed and in the role! The result was an extremely rewarding adventure directing an educational program for older adults on a college campus. It actually was "my job." But I was coming back to a non-profit agency I already had familiarity/connections with. So, I suppose a stealth approach works for retreading former work environments as well!

After a few years, I transitioned to another non-profit. Fast-forward another few years, and I am stealth networking yet again, but this time into the for-profit senior service world.

Knowing a few people at the networking meetings I attend, I asked them to introduce me to whomever they thought I should meet. Any doubt I had regarding making the leap from the non-profit to the for-profit world rapidly dissipated because of what I saw about how the stealth method works.

A woman who was an instructor for me in the senior educational program introduced me to someone immediately who arranged to interview me the next day. That job wasn't right for me, but a few weeks later, I interviewed for one that was. The same career tribe member had made this connection for me as well. In just a few weeks, I will be celebrating my one year anniversary working for that company. Think positive, and never underestimate the power of your lifetime network. You can do it!

Dawn Muroff
Life Enrichment Director
Emeritus of Chatsworth
www.emeritus.com

STEALTH DISCOVERY OF A BUSINESS OPPORTUNITY

I've spent 28 years in the banking business. In my last position, I was the marketing director for a payments software company. I left that last employer in late 2008 in a force reduction action that trimmed the staff of our payments software company by about 20 percent. This happened because our market was major banks that, at the time, were struggling with their own huge financial problems at the beginning of the recession. They were spending no money whatsoever on software.

In that economic climate, I decided to rethink my approach to searching for a job. As a result, I sought a career coach and landed on the stealth method. Fairly quickly, I was having stealth interviews in various fields that I had considered moving into. It was empowering to have a tool that allowed me to connect and get information on a wide variety of interests.

The area I was most drawn to was the application of business intelligence techniques to banking and financial services. I had always managed my staff using key measures of performance. The advantage of using key measures is that they clearly communicate what is important so the staff can be creative in deciding how to achieve our business goals. This simplifies the management process and creates a much better work environment. It demonstrates the core process of business intelligence: to identify the key performance indicators (KPIs in industry jargon) and create a way to reliably measure and report this information.

One of my stealth research projects was to explore the potential need for business intelligence techniques in banking, and one particular meeting was with a retired bank president. I asked a broad question in the beginning of the interview that centered on my interest: "What is the most important management information you were lacking as a bank president?" The answer was totally unexpected. He said he never knew the cash flow of his customers on a timely basis, which is what a bank relies on for loan payment. He went on to explain to me that the information he and every banker gets is weeks or even months old because it is taken from the financial statements provided by the customer which, of course, are historical documents.

Having just left a payments software company, I knew there was a way to provide this information on a daily basis through automation. The stealth approach had shown me a new business opportunity.

I continued to use the stealth method to perform additional research to determine if there was a real business opportunity in this idea. It led me to meet with a large number of bankers and credit consultants, all of whom confirmed the real value in the concept. Not only was I getting the information and confirmation I needed, but I was even establishing a ready client base in the process. The result is that I launched a company to provide this service in late 2010.

As I sell the service idea to bankers, I continually find that applying the stealth techniques I learned opens doors to high-level meetings and valuable discussions. It is when I stop using the techniques out of laziness that I get into trouble!

Bob Merkle

CEO, Cash Flow Insights

www.cashflowinsights.com

Appendix B: Career Transformation Affirmations

The process of exploring your passions and then finding and connecting with individuals who will lead to opportunities outlined in this book works. It's been proven time and again by folks who faithfully engage in the discipline involved. Sure, you can always revert back to the standard, overt approach, which is definitely a lot easier. But if it's actual results that you want—those results being the establishing of a huge network of connections that can serve to continuously guide you along your path to opportunities both inside and outside your current field, then this stealth method is the way to go.

Sometimes, however, our old stinkin' thinkin' about not being that special, or having nothing we're really passionate about, or being a bother to people who for sure would never have time for us (gag!) can get in the way. Therefore, to support you in realigning your belief structure in such a way as to create an internal environment (meaning your *heart* and *mind*) conducive to a successful stealth campaign, I've compiled some helpful affirmations.

The way an affirmation works is this: you repeat it several times a day, perhaps morning, noon, and night. This is a must while you're actually in search mode, and always helpful just to lift your spirits. First, your internal voice may scoff at them, say they are silly, and say that you are silly for even repeating them to yourself. That's the same internal critic, however, that would tell you that you can never do anything other than what you've done, that you're too old, that you can't really make a total career change, or start a business, or get known by the power players, or...blah, blah, blah. On and on it goes, telling you how limited and inconsequential you are.

But, as you repeat these affirmations regularly, and begin to allow yourself to even entertain their veracity, you will start seeing signs in the world that they are true. Someone makes time for you whom you would never have expected. Someone refers you to another individual who opens up doors you could have never dreamed of. People remember you and call you when opportunities arise that you may be interested in. And, slowly but surely, as you continue to affirm this world you would *like to be true*, it actually becomes true...because you replaced that old, stinkin' thinkin' with a more beautiful and fragrant world view.

CAREER TRANSITION AFFIRMATIONS

☞ I have important knowledge, skill, and talent to share.

☞ I add value to the workplace.

☞ I bring a unique essence to every situation I touch.

☞ I am a worthwhile and sought-after individual.

☞ I honor and speak the highest truth about myself.

☞ I proudly promote myself, because I am good at what I do.

☞ My unique career essence can be expressed in multiple ways, and I discover more every day.

☞ I easily open doors into my every field of interest.

☞ People want to assist me, and I joyously invite and allow them to.

☞ I am amazed at how much people want to contribute to me.

☞ My job is to build and maintain relationships, and perfect employment takes care of itself.

☞ I easily attract career opportunities I truly love.

NOTE: Download a copy of these affirmations suitable for framing at *www.careerguy.com*

Index

About the Author

Darrell Gurney is a 25-year veteran of career support and a licensed spiritual counselor. He has coached and supported thousands in making profitable, fulfilling career transitions or building thriving businesses. After 15 years as an executive recruiter, he authored the award-winning book *Headhunters Revealed: Career Secrets for Choosing and Using Professional Recruiters*, which was reviewed in *Publishers Weekly* and won the Clarion Award for Best Book from the Association for Women in Communications.

In *Never Apply for a Job Again!*, Darrell takes off the recruiter hat and places it firmly on your head…so that you can now become your own effective career manager for life. As a headhunter, he gave you a fish—a job. Now he teaches you *how* to fish.

He is the founder of CareerGuy.com, a frequent speaker at professional events, and a contributor to the media in the area of job search and career development. He has consulted for top organizations within the outplacement industry and also consults private corporations in the areas of staff and team development. His purpose is to elicit freedom and aliveness so that people and organizations can create inspired new futures.

Darrell is an avid writer, personal development sponge, outdoors aficionado, high-adventure junkie, karaoke addict, and his son's assistant scoutmaster. He is currently completing his next book about mid-life empowerment and purposeful fulfillment in the second half of life, *The Back Forty: 7 Critical Embraces for Life's Purposeful Second Half.* He lives and works in Los Angeles, California.

Also from CAREER PRESS

WINNING JOB INTERVIEWS
Revised Edition
Paul Powers
EAN 978-1601630889

WORK AT HOME NOW
Christine Durst & Michael Haaren
EAN 978-1601630919

HIGHLY EFFECTIVE
NETWORKING
Orville Pierson
EAN 978-1601630506

NO-NONSENSE RESUMES
Wendy Enelow & Arnold Boldt
EAN 978-1564149053

Also from CAREER PRESS

100 WAYS TO
MOTIVATE YOURSELF
Revised Edition
Steve Chandler
EAN 978-1564147752

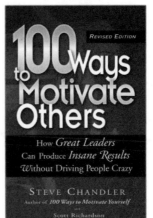

100 WAYS TO
MOTIVATE OTHERS
Revised Edition
Steve Chandler
EAN 978-1564149923

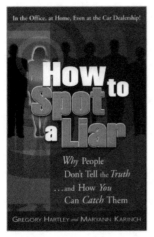

HOW TO SPOT A LIAR
Gregory Hartley &
Maryann Karinch
EAN 978-1564148407

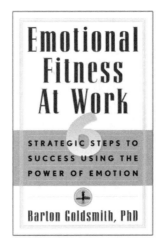

EMOTIONAL FITNESS AT WORK
Barton Goldsmith
EAN 978-1601630810

TO ORDER CALL 1-800-227-3371 OR VISIT CAREERPRESS.COM